Citizen Journalism

Citizen Journalism explores citizen participation in the news as an evolving disruptive practice in digital journalism. This volume moves beyond the debates over the mainstream news media attempts to control and contain citizen journalism to focus attention in a different direction: the peripheries of traditional journalism. Here, more independent forms of citizen journalism, enabled by social media, are creating their own forms of news.

Among the actors at the boundaries of the professional journalism field the book identifies are the engaged citizen journalist and the enraged citizen journalist. The former consists of under-represented voices leading social justice movements, while the latter reflects the views of conservatives and the alt-right, who often view citizen journalism as a performance. *Citizen Journalism* further explores how non-journalism arenas, such as citizen science, enable ordinary citizens to collect data and become protectors of the environment.

Citizen Journalism serves as an important reminder of the professional field's failure to effectively respond to the changing nature of public communication. These changes have helped to create new spaces for new actors; in such places, traditional as well as upstart forms of journalism negotiate and compete, ultimately aiding the journalism field in creating its future.

Melissa Wall is a professor in the Department of Journalism at California State University, Northridge, USA. She is the author of *Citizen Journalism: Valuable, Useless or Dangerous?* and founder of the Pop-Up Newsroom.

Disruptions: Studies in Digital Journalism
Series editor: Bob Franklin

Disruptions refers to the radical changes provoked by the affordances of digital technologies that occur at a pace and on a scale that disrupt settled understandings and traditional ways of creating value, interacting and communicating both socially and professionally. The consequences for digital journalism involve far reaching changes to business models, professional practices, roles, ethics, products and even challenges to the accepted definitions and understandings of journalism. For digital journalism studies, the field of academic inquiry which explores and examines digital journalism, disruption results in paradigmatic and tectonic shifts in scholarly concerns. It prompts reconsideration of research methods, theoretical analyses and responses (oppositional and consensual) to such changes, which have been described as being akin to 'a moment of mind blowing uncertainty'.

Routledge's new book series, *Disruptions: Studies in Digital Journalism*, seeks to capture, examine and analyse these moments of exciting and explosive professional and scholarly innovation which characterize developments in the day-to-day practice of journalism in an age of digital media, and which are articulated in the newly emerging academic discipline of digital journalism studies.

Disrupting Journalism Ethics
Stephen J. A. Ward

Social Media Livestreaming
Claudette G. Artwick

Citizen Journalism: Practices, Propaganda, Pedagogy
Melissa Wall

Data Journalism and the Regeneration of News
Alfred Hermida and Mary Lynn Young

www.routledge.com/Disruptions/book-series/DISRUPTDIGJOUR

Citizen Journalism
Practices, Propaganda, Pedagogy

Melissa Wall

Routledge
Taylor & Francis Group

LONDON AND NEW YORK

First published 2019 by Routledge

2 Park Square, Milton Park, Abingdon, Oxon OX14 4RN
605 Third Avenue, New York, NY 10017

Routledge is an imprint of the Taylor & Francis Group, an informa business

First issued in paperback 2022

Publisher's Note

The publisher has gone to great lengths to ensure the quality of this reprint but points out that some imperfections in the original copies may be apparent.

British Library Cataloguing-in-Publication Data
A catalogue record for this book is available from the British Library

Library of Congress Cataloging-in-Publication Data
Names: Wall, Melissa, author.
Title: Citizen journalism : practices, propaganda, pedagogy / Melissa Wall.
Description: London ; New York, NY : Routledge, 2019. | Series: Disruptions: studies in digital journalism | Includes bibliographical references and index.
Identifiers: LCCN 2018048104 (print) | LCCN 2018056837 (ebook) | ISBN 9781351055703 (ebook) | ISBN 9781138483156 (hardback : alk. paper)
Subjects: LCSH: Citizen journalism. | Online journalism. | Social media.
Classification: LCC PN4784.C615 (ebook) | LCC PN4784.C615 W35 2019 (print) | DDC 070.4/3—dc23
LC record available at https://lccn.loc.gov/2018048104

ISBN: 978-1-138-48315-6 (hbk)
ISBN: 978-1-03-233865-1 (pbk)
DOI: 10.4324/9781351055703

Typeset in Times New Roman
by Apex CoVantage, LLC

Contents

Acknowledgments

My understanding of the issues addressed in this volume began with field-work at the WTO protests in Seattle, which birthed the Independent Media Center. My thinking was further shaped by the journalists I interviewed as a Fulbright Scholar at Notre Dame University in Lebanon when citizen journalism from the Syrian conflict was just beginning to draw our attention. Likewise, scholars from the Mohyla School of Journalism in Ukraine, where I was an Open Society International Scholar, alerted me to the ways citizen news could be freighted with misinformation and manipulated into propaganda.

I am particularly grateful to the thoughtful guidance of Disruptions Series Editor Bob Franklin, who made this volume possible. A grant from the Mike Curb College of Arts, Media and Communication at California State University – Northridge afforded me valuable time to research and write. Journalism Department Chair Linda Bowen provided unwavering support, while Elizabeth Blakey, Stephanie Bluestein and Paromita Pain read drafts of the manuscript. As always, Bronwyn Mauldin's unflagging belief in whatever I do was my propellant throughout this process.

1   Introduction: Citizen journalism at the margins

"They are shooting at us with grenades, grenade launchers, snipers," says a bloodied Oscar Pérez, staring into a shaky camera as he films himself. Bangs from weapons shook the screen. Another man off camera somewhere else in the house shouts, "We have families we want to see." Pérez and six others who wanted to overthrow the Venezuelan government were holed up in a safe house on the outskirts of Caracas in the middle of a shootout with government security forces in early 2018.

A former police officer and one-time action film actor, the blue-eyed, blond Pérez was already known to authorities and citizens alike as what the international news media described as a sort of "James Bond" or "Rambo" (Lozano, 2017, para. 1; Venezuela Says Rebel Pilot Oscar Perez Killed in Raid, 2018, para. 21). As protests rocked his country in the summer of 2017, Pérez had stolen a government helicopter from which he lobbed stun grenades at Venezuela's Supreme Court. Six months later, he and a group of masked men captured a National Guard post and smashed photos of Venezuela's president Nicolas Maduro and former president Hugo Chavez, an action Pérez filmed and posted to his YouTube account.

The Caracas shootout was also documented on social media. A cell phone video taken from within the neighborhood where the rebels were hiding shows security forces crouching behind the walls of other homes. Tweets and Instagram posts from citizens in the immediate area as well as from members of the security forces surrounding the rebels were posted online (see Venezuelan Rebel Leader Oscar Pérez Records His Last Stand, 2018). Some show an explosion at the safe house, plumes of smoke obscuring what exactly was happening. So it was that the last hours of Oscar Pérez's life were fodder for citizen journalism. That we can watch such an event as it happens has come to be expected. What makes this case of citizens using social media to report on a dramatic event different is what happened next: This content became part of the source material of an unofficial investigation into what actually happened at the safe house.

An organization founded by former citizen journalist Eliot Higgins decided to collaboratively scrutinize the existing evidence on whether Pérez was given a chance to surrender or whether he and his companions were executed by government forces. Higgins had started out as an anonymous blogger interested in identifying bombs in Syria; he eventually became a skilled investigator, using social media and other open source materials to identify the precise weapons used and their origins. From these experiences, Higgins formed Bellingcat, a collaborative, citizen-fueled investigative organization operating on "a shoestring budget, using social media and satellite photography, and tapping into a network of obsessives" (Pollack, 2017, para. 21). Bellingcat was instrumental in identifying Russia as ultimately responsible for shooting down the Malaysian passenger plane MH17/MAS17 over Ukraine in 2014, resulting in the deaths of 283 passengers and 15 crew members. In the Pérez investigation, Bellingcat joined forces with Forensic Architecture, an innovative interdisciplinary research agency based at Goldsmiths, University of London, to investigate the Pérez shootout. Together, they began collecting citizen-generated media content, asking for the public's help in determining what happened. Representatives from the two organizations explained their thinking: "New investigative techniques allow citizens and researchers to find the truth when the government wants to hide it. But to do that we need evidence"; they believed citizens would be able to provide it (Fiorella & Leroy, 2018).

Bellingcat in particular models an evolving dynamic in journalism, in which new citizen news collectors position themselves at the borders of the journalism field and engage in journalistic practices. To complicate this example, the call for help and a presentation of existing evidence appeared in an article authored by Bellingcat and Forensic Architecture in the online editorial section of the *New York Times*, demonstrating the fluidity of boundaries between amateur and professional journalists. In this way, the citizen upstarts can help the sometimes slower-moving profession to connect to innovative projects where unexpected ways of performing journalism may thrive. These nimble newcomers offer creative re-imaginings of how information may be collaboratively collected and assessed. As will be laid out in this volume, particularly active citizen journalists along with news apprentices and non-journalists are participating in the production of public information today. Some of these new types of citizen journalists may have little desire to be incorporated into the mainstream news field. Others may ultimately seek the demise of traditional news as practiced today.

Competing definitions of citizen journalism

Different environments for citizen journalism have contributed to the debate over who citizen journalists are and what citizen journalism is.

Some suggest citizen journalists are unpaid variants on professional journalists who nevertheless follow the rules of the road ("semi-professional amateurs"), while others assert that citizen journalists are those who don't have the time to fully report the news, and who lack the technical abilities or knowledge to produce a coherent story (Bock, 2012; Kim & Lowrey, 2015; Nicey, 2016; Allan, 2015). Scholars remind us that that citizen journalists are often ordinary people who happen to be present when extraordinary events take place and thus are simply "accidental" bystanders (Harrison, 2010, p. 245). Overall, as Dahlgren (2016) notes, citizen journalism "resists easy definition or unified history" (p. 215).

Observers of the genre do not agree on whether citizen journalism is even the appropriate term to describe the participation of amateurs in the news; hence, we see a range of terms used: participatory journalism, grassroots journalism and so forth (see Nip, 2006, for typology). Indeed, finding an agreed-upon name is difficult because citizen journalism is often viewed as the purview of professional journalism, and many professional news outlets don't even use the term citizen journalism. They opt instead for other appellations, such as UGC or crowd-sourced content, seeing citizen journalism as a phenomenon primarily to be tamed or managed. This prominence of professional journalists in defining citizen news normalizes the idea that they determine how it is responded to, placing this new genre within certain constraints and ultimately limiting its possibilities. Ironically, another key point of debate in defining citizen journalism is the argument that it can be citizen journalism only if it is occurring outside the structures of mainstream news media (Kim & Lowrey, 2015). Yet it has become increasingly difficult to consider citizen journalism separately from traditional journalism because of the rise of social media platforms where citizen content appears alongside professional news in hybrid information spaces that audiences do not necessarily distinguish between (Hermida, 2015, 2016).

There is also the tendency to view citizen journalists as one-off contributors – those at the "right place at the right time" as Rodriguez puts it (2014, p. 205). This fails to reflect that some of them are not new to the production of news. Studies of those who create citizen journalism demonstrate that there is a continuum of contributors, some with no experience but also former journalists, journalism students and others who work professionally in adjacent fields, such as nonprofits that produce media content (Ahva, 2017; Kus, Eberwein, Porlezza, & Splendore, 2017). Ahva (2017, p. 142) calls these contributors "in-betweeners," who are performing in a liminal state that exists between full-time professionals and clueless amateurs committing one-off acts of journalism. Their participation may do more than merely document. For some citizen journalists, it may help build community, sustain public debates or contribute to their personal development.

Some researchers have argued that due to this incoherence we should focus on what citizen journalists do rather than who they are – not the label for the person but the label for the practices in which they engage (Bock, 2012; Domingo & Le Cam, 2016). But even here, there is not a shared meaning. What citizen journalism is depends on the local context in which it is produced as well as the contexts of reception. Citizen journalism in different regions of the world, including those countries with a lack of information freedom under oppressive governments, has taken root in different soil. Consider the ways citizen journalism in non-Western countries has challenged authoritarian rule, sometimes becoming an identity used to represent resistance to the powers that be in ways that could prove dangerous for those who are so labeled. This is well illustrated with the citizen journalism produced during the Arab Spring. Prado (2017) argues that much citizen journalism in the Global South "privileges the perspective of communities and populations underrepresented in legacy news media accounts: this reporting may reaffirm cultural identity or chronicle the everyday life of rural, isolated or disenfranchised populations, or of cultures nearing extinction" (p. 89). Of course, these same efforts of resistance and representation can be found in the West. Thus, there is no one form of citizen journalism but many iterations based on the context and actors involved. Around the world and even within individual countries, citizen journalism is not a unified set of practices. While photographs of sunsets or comments about celebrities may be considered forms of citizen journalism in some contexts, in this volume, part of the focus is on forms of activist-oriented citizen journalism. Such content is often produced within a network of like-minded others, whose goals are to create social and political change. Thus, I define citizen journalism here as the production of original media content by amateurs and other in-betweeners that aims to contribute to the building of community and sometimes to social change.

Placing citizen journalism

Citizen journalism is by now a well-researched topic with many of the key issues debated and discussed across various volumes and special issues (see Allan, 2015; Allan & Thorsen, 2009; Rosenberry & St. John, 2009; Thorsen & Allan, 2014; Wall, 2012, 2016, 2017). Such examinations frequently focus on the reception of citizen journalism by professional journalists, stressing the ways mainstream journalism has well-developed routines for incorporating citizen journalism into its news (Borger, Van Hoof, & Sanders, 2016b; Canter, 2013; Domingo, 2011; Robinson, 2009). Some research finds citizens are gladly invited to participate in the professional media outlets' production of the news, although oftentimes within highly structured forms used to segregate or diminish citizen contributions (Wahl-Jorgensen, 2015; Li & Hellmueller, 2016). Other analysis suggests that there is actually not so much citizen involvement in mainstream news but instead more of an illusion of participation that helps professional journalists to maintain real control over the news (Jönsson & Örnebring, 2011; Karlsson, 2011; Karlsson, Bergström, Clerwall, & Fast, 2015). In many cases, the aim appears to be to introduce such limited participation that it does not lessen the authority of the professionals (Singer, 2015).

In this book, I shift attention away from this foundational research that positions citizen journalists as reluctantly accepted guests at the doors of traditional journalism, often gaining entry only by invitation, and instead focus mainly on citizen journalism on the peripheries of the professional journalism field. In his analysis of new digital journalism actors, Eldridge (2018) identified this area as key to our understanding of journalism today. These margins are where a diverse range of actors compete to be heard, sometimes finding meeting points with the guardians of the discipline and/or each other and sometimes not. Such actors may initiate their own entry into the field in hopes of achieving the competencies expected by the professionals. Others may find themselves at the edges of the journalism, having emerged from entirely different fields.

In these margins, power is more dispersed and the profession itself less secure. These metaphoric borderlands are liminal spaces that are "unpredictable and transitional" (Anzaldua, 1987, p. 243). Thinking in terms of the edges of the profession is important because here practices and values are fluid and unstable and thus seemingly more hospitable to transformations, engendering new connections and possibilities. At the periphery, we find an increasingly permeable space sometimes mingling mainstream, traditional journalism with the content produced by various other actors, including a spectrum of different types of citizen journalists. To understand these border areas and the actors assembled there, scholars have increasingly turned to two associated bodies of research – field theory and professional boundary work – to guide our thinking (Bourdieu, 1993, 2005; Benson, 2013; Benson & Neveu, 2005; Carlson, 2015; Eldridge, 2018; Lewis, 2015; Robinson, 2010; Singer, 2015).

Bourdieu (2005) argues that journalism exists as a "field" or a social space with its own rules and practices in which actors compete for symbolic and cultural resources. As a field, journalism has its own habitus, which consists of "encompassing ideological predispositions, judgments of taste and physical bearing shaped by family, education and profession" (Benson, 2013, p. 27). Specifically, the habitus of traditional journalism is seen in formulaic writing practices, such as quoting sources and attribution of information. Journalistic habitus is also evident in the practice of relying on the power elite for information as a way to establish credibility (Robinson, 2015). Those in the know are able to indicate their belonging and status in the field through the display of these dispositions. For Bourdieu, an institutional or professional field is a site of struggle. Thus, fields are constantly striving against external threats from other fields as well as internal threats from actors seeking to gain power for themselves.

A second, related area of research focuses on the ways limits are established within professions through the study of boundary work, which operates to keep insiders in power and to exclude outsiders (Carlson, 2015; Lewis, 2015). To draw boundaries is to establish and reinforce a profession's legitimacy and authority. Since journalism does not have the same sort of official credentials as professions such as medicine or law, whose practitioners may be certified by taking examinations, it has relied instead on an accepted body of practices. Such rules for journalism traditionally include objectivity and distance in reporting as well as a journalist's presence at the site of news making (Singer, 2015). These accepted norms, which are known both internally and externally to the field, establish what journalism is, aiming to maintain it as a particular, special type of public communication (Hermida, 2015).

Mainstream news media have been successful in the last decade at creating practices that highlight boundaries between themselves and "interlopers," new actors often claiming to be journalists or at least having the right to practice journalism as they interpret it (Eldridge, 2018, p. 2). The insiders both diminish and contain the outsiders and also at times offer them some benefits, such as amplifying their content. For example, when CNN uses citizen video, the global newscaster may provide the creator with possible access to an enormous audience but will also make certain that audiences are cued to see it as possibly suspect and unprofessional, as less than what a professional would create (Pantti & Andén-Papadopoulos, 2011). Lewis (2012) has called this the competing impulses toward open participation versus control. While some professional news organizations attempt to collaborate with the producers of citizen content, they still exercise ultimate gatekeeping for much of the information in the public sphere (Canter, 2013; Singer, 2015; Wall & el Zahed, 2015). In examples from around the world, we see these attempts by mainstream news entities to both recognize and make use of citizen journalism but also to control the genre. For example, Singapore's the *Straits Times'* Stomp site describes itself as "activating Singapore's most awesome citizen journalists," which is accomplished through submitting content to a special, segregated section of its website. In other words, it is limiting participation to spaces away from the main news site. Other news organizations follow the example of the *Times of India*, which created a special app called the "Citizen Reporter," which encourages ordinary people to use the app to share stories and articulate opinions. The app sends their contributions to the news outlet, which considers what is of value. While often accused of soliciting free labor, such initiatives mainly work to maintain the primacy of traditional, particularly corporate, journalism, setting the terms for what will be submitted and what will be done with it once they have the contributed content in hand. In doing so, professionals both contain the amateurs and offer what may seem to be some attractive benefits: amplifying citizen voices and sharing some of their credibility.

Into this networked communication environment have come social media that allow some citizen journalists to ignore the core of the field and instead to flourish in the border areas, potentially making news in new and disruptive ways. As seen in the Oscar Pérez example, new actors are carrying out the sorts of investigations that are traditionally the domain of professional journalists. They are deploying some of the idealized traditional values of established journalism (finding out the truth, questioning government actions) and also relying on new ones, such as calls for the public to crowdsource evidence. In this way, these newcomers draw on competencies that are different from the traditional routes necessary to achieve success within the field. In this fluid space between old and new actors, the boundaries of the field, particularly once they are made evident by the actions of the outsiders, may shift (Eldridge, 2016; Robinson, 2015). The project by Bellingcat and Forensic Architecture demonstrates how previous journalistic markers of expertise are being joined by other values and practices in a connected world in which new forms of accountability and transparency may develop (Hermida, 2015). As Eldridge (2016) notes, "emerging digital actors pursuing journalistic work have irritated and blurred the traditional boundaries of the journalistic field" (p. 44). Indeed, Bellingcat's Higgins says that while his organization publishes articles, "what we're focusing on is not publishing an article as a journalistic endeavor . . . we're publishing it to summarize data we've collected from investigations into certain types of incidents" (Sullivan, 2017, para. 10). This is quite a step beyond the type of content some news organizations' citizen sites solicit, such as asking audiences to submit a photograph of a car wreck or to describe a travel hot spot.

While the Bellingcat collaboration suggests an intriguing reinvention of journalism, choosing to work with professional journalists means citizen-originated projects – however sophisticated and creative – may still not be fully legitimized because the traditional news media will want to maintain authority. With the Pérez project, the *New York Times* lent its credibility along with access to its more than 250 million online viewers. This is a clear acknowledgment of the perceived need to work with these new actors in some capacity; yet, it is also a means of keeping actors like Bellingcat and Forensic Architecture under the watchful eyes of the professionals.

The Pérez article is in fact placed on the *New York Times* opinion pages, which signals to audiences that it has been incorporated into the publication but still lies outside the hard news pages, where most investigations would appear. As Carlson (2015, p. 7) notes, "boundaries stress limits" and we can also say consistency, as agreed-upon values and practices appear to be necessary for a field to continue to exist as it currently is. However, the resulting uniformity is also potentially debilitating, as Dickinson et al. (2012) argue that diversity, rather than homogeneity, is more often the impetus for innovation. Constancy of practice could make it difficult to meet the challenges of communicating public information, leading to the weakening or even demise of the field.

Outline of the book

While the enactment of citizen journalism remains a veritable kaleidoscope of actions and expectations, with some exceptions, much of this book focuses on citizen journalism practices in the United States. Additional examples from around the world are also drawn on for contrast and deeper understanding with the understanding that its forms may be quite different depending on the specific political and historical context of the country in which they take place (Prado, 2017).

Chapter 2 focuses on what I call the engaged citizen journalist, an outsider who produces news or informational content that may serve the interests of the oppressed, amplifying their voices and concerns. Their journalism is often independent of traditional news structures and, in some cases, they express no desire to be normalized, preferring instead to be on the margins of the professional field (Kus et al., 2017). In doing so, they "interrupt conventional discussions about journalism borders" (Bock, 2016, p. 14). This is an important area to consider because engaged citizen journalism has often been undermined by professionals and overlooked by scholars despite its practitioners' active involvement with important social and political issues in ways that motivate them to provide sustained coverage (Chadha & Steiner, 2015).

Chapter 3 describes the enraged citizen journalist, who often aims to incubate dissensus, conflict and rage, oftentimes by creating misinformation. Here, unsanctioned citizen news practitioners appear to be contributing to societal conflicts. In the cases of self-described citizen journalists such as Andrew Breitbart of *Breitbart News*, their actions also cleave the boundaries of traditional journalism, challenging the field in ways that are unruly, unpredictable and not necessarily working for the public good. The ways enraged citizen journalists can activate nationalism and populist anger have been the subject of a small body of work mainly on non-Western countries, such as China or Syria (see Al Ghazzi, 2014; Reese & Dai, 2009). In countries with historically high levels of freedom of speech, such as the United States, such consideration is more rare. Yet today concerns about disinformation and propaganda have become more crucial, and this chapter focuses on how outsiders to mainstream news are playing roles in these processes through the claiming of a certain type of citizen journalism identity and sometimes through an emotive performance of that identity.

While some at the margins of the profession actively claim the identity of journalist, others carry out citizen journalistic practices from other fields entirely. Chapter 4 focuses on forms of citizen participation in the collection and reporting of information and/or creative content in the non-journalistic arenas of science and the arts, finding the former excels at enabling ordinary people to participate. Meanwhile, the arts, as with journalism, struggles between impulses to collaborate for social change and impulses to collaborate for financial gain. Another peripheral area explored in Chapter 5 consists of initiatives to train citizen journalists. Some efforts are thin – the posting of self-directed tutorials online – while others consist of face-to-face sessions that build trust and possibly incubate reciprocal relationships. Are these spaces merely used to socialize citizen journalists and maintain control over the field's norms or are they the means to help expand the field's understanding of itself? Or are they both? Using Lave and Wenger's (1991/2003) concept of legitimate peripheral participation, I offer an analytical framework for thinking about the schooling of citizen journalists and the ways this might strengthen the field or at least contribute to experiments in its margins. The book concludes with Chapter 6, which identifies missed opportunities to create a more robust journalistic community and argues that journalism as we have known it is being not merely disrupted but challenged in ways that may permanently alter or even replace current understandings.

Conclusion

Independent forms of citizen and other types of participatory journalism continue to expand not merely because of technological changes but due to the failures of professional news to adequately respond to the changing nature of how people participate in public communication. Professional journalism has often failed to bring citizens closer to the news, instead keeping them at a distance. In fact, communities that traditional journalism purports to represent often express a sense of distrust and even fear of professional journalists (Palmer, 2017). The news industry's "Olympian" view of the audience (Dahlgren, 2016, p. 251), which is particularly true of the largest, most influential outlets, decides who is recognized and validated, and who remains invisible to the broader public. Indeed, as Anderson (2013) argues, the norm for many years has been that journalists have no idea who their audiences are. Many citizen journalists intentionally reject this drawing of a line between themselves and the public, on whose trust they depend. Thus, this book serves as a reminder that the professional field's failures to effectively respond helped to create new spaces for new actors and that the margins may be the sites where not only new and old forms of journalism negotiate and compete but also new identities come into being and the journalism field itself will possibly find a future.

2   Engaged citizen journalism

The grainy video shows a line of dark-clad law enforcement officers, faces hidden behind helmet visors. The camera is held by Eric Poemoceah, a citizen journalist who is telling the police that "six thousand one hundred people" are watching what they are doing here on a muddy road cutting through snow-covered hills in Standing Rock, ND, in the early winter of 2017. Thousands of activists and water protectors have gathered here to try to stop the laying of the Dakota Access Pipeline, which will pollute the water, destroy sacred lands and violate Native American treaty rights with the U.S. government.

The line of police surges toward the crowd and protesters' footfalls can be heard as they try to scramble away. The screen becomes blurry and Poemoceah yells, "My hip, my hip" after he has apparently been shoved to the ground. The live-streamed video posted to his Facebook page is picked up by television station News6 in Tulsa, Oklahoma, near his hometown, and appears online with the caption, "Lawton native Eric Poemoceah was arrested yesterday in Bismarck, N.D., as a part of the Dakota Access pipeline protest and he streamed the whole thing on Facebook" (n.d.). Professional journalist Scott Rains (2017), in his sympathetic story in the *Lawton Constitution*, writes that Poemoceah's video

> documented the walk through soggy conditions around the camp and over a bridge that crossed onto federal land. The day's wind and snow/rain mix marked harsh surroundings. He complained that electronic communications were being jammed at different times. He mentioned a lone American flag, flying upside down in the husk of a camp as a symbol of a nation in distress against the pipeline. He offered reverence to the assorted teepees and tents that had been blessed and home to countless ceremonies.
>
> "I didn't come here to get arrested, I came here to protect the water," Poemoceah said in the video.
>
> (para. 8)

Like others at the Standing Rock encampment, Poemoceah was both "a self-styled citizen journalist" documenting events as they unfolded and a participant in the actions to oppose the pipeline (Rains, 2017, para. 1). In one video, he panned across a group of protesters along the edge of the river with police gathered above them on a bluff on the other side. Poemoceah says, "This is a stand. We're not taking it no more from you DAPL."

A member of the group Comanches in Motion, he had traveled from Oklahoma to be part of the movement to protect Native land from energy and oil corporations. In 2016–17 thousands of protesters, including indigenous people from all over the United States and the rest of the Americas, social justice activists, environmentalists, youth, celebrities and others simply curious or looking for trouble made their way to Standing Rock to challenge, protest, witness and, in the case of citizen journalists such as Poemoceah, report on what was happening. Like him, many used social media, often live streaming on Facebook, to share their stories. Amateur journalists such as Poemoceah independently documented what they saw and, as in the intense moments described earlier, were amplified on occasion by the mainstream news media, which have been criticized for failing to pay much attention to the initial story (Franco, 2017). In one video, he conducts a friendly interview with two local reporters, who demur when he asks if they support his cause.

His actions embody a type of amateur journalist – the engaged citizen journalist, who is independent of the mainstream news media in terms of reporting and posting his or her own versions of events and is supportive of actions for social change. Like many others, he works within connective information networks that sometimes intertwine amateurs and professionals in increasingly complex ways. As Alfred Hermida (2016, p. 407) explains about the rise of social media as information platforms, "News, information and comment [circulate] outside of the established order and hierarchy associated with traditional print or broadcast structures." Just as protesters may gather and occupy physical spaces, citizen journalists have "occupied the media, or in the vocabulary of the era of the computer code, they 'hacked the news,'" demonstrating how they create their own news networks and bypass traditional news institutions (Russell, 2016, p. 3).

Most of the engaged citizen journalists are not accidental bystanders or random witnesses who happen to capture a snippet of content. They often chose to be present at scenes of political and social conflict. They make their own judgments concerning what to document, which may or may not resemble mainstream news choices. They are sympathetic to or even participants in the events they cover. These engaged citizen journalists increasingly document movements (and sometimes more ephemeral moments) involving social issues, such as racial inequality and white domination or what Waisbord (2014) calls "social change news" (p. 189). While some are on site documenting the actions for days or longer, a secondary form of engaged citizen journalism takes place when ordinary people capture unanticipated acts of oppression on screen with the specific intent to document and share this content in order to challenge and publicly call out their perpetrators. In particular, communities that have not been appropriately represented or found themselves not represented at all – indigenous people whose land is taken from them, African Americans who are harassed or killed for no reason, and others – send this content through their own information networks from where it may sometimes be injected into larger, more general information spheres. In their study of Black Twitter and other similar social media groupings for Asian Americans and feminists, Freelon, Lopez, Clark and Jackson (2018, p. 7) found members of marginalized communities "have assumed the role of news creators and distributors . . . producing their own news." Similarly, Allissa Richardson (2017) argues that Twitter is "African Americans' preferred ad hoc new millennium news outlet" (p. 674).

While research suggests the mainstream journalists devote considerable efforts to distinguishing themselves from these interlopers into public information spaces, many of these engaged citizen journalists show little desire to be schooled by the mainstream news media (Eldridge, 2018; Wall, 2018). They are operating within new information networks that rely on dispersed ties, often formed with strangers and pulled together in part by the affordances of social media platforms. Such networks can diminish the importance of professional journalists, who become a "peripheral rather than a central node" for news or are even "rendered surprisingly irrelevant" (Bossio & Bebawi, 2012; DeLuca & Lawson, 2014, p. 369; Robinson & Schwartz, 2014, p. 386).

This chapter concentrates on these new actors and the production of their own news, shifting our attention from the usual questions of how the mainstream news media claim authority and protect their positions within the journalism field. Instead, this discussion focuses on the boundary areas that exist between professionals and these engaged amateurs. Here, change percolates, shaping new modes of journalism as citizen journalists create alternative news accounts of important events, experiment with technologies and practices, and contribute to what Russell (2016) argues is the movement of professional journalism closer to activism in their reportage. These engaged citizen journalists are often allied with social media–savvy groups connected to diverse communities, such as the indigenous-led opposition in Standing Rock, Black Lives Matter and youth-led immigration activism around the Dreamers and other undocumented people. This diversity is important to recognize as Western citizen journalism has been accused of favoring white voices (Mahrouse, 2012). In fact, although generating less research attention, the role of citizen journalism within ethnic media, which have a long history of supporting advocacy work on their behalf, may be a prototype of engaged citizen journalists.

Practices of engaged citizen journalism

In what follows, I identify key characteristics of engaged citizen journalism that tend to support activism. In addition to the water protectors, the undocumented and other resistance examples, I draw particularly on the ways citizen journalists have covered the repeated cases of unarmed African Americans being abused or even killed by police. Included here as well are other incidents that were not responses to state violence but to individual acts of aggression against African Americans in the spring and summer of 2018 that have been documented and distributed in what a *New Yorker* (2018) headline calls, "The Summer of Coupon Carl, Permit Patty, and the Videos That Turn White Privilege into Mockable Memes" (St. Félix, 2018). In these ways, African Americans now "report news independently with their cellphones," creating an "unapologetic form of advocacy journalism" (Richardson, 2017, p. 2). Indeed, research confirms that the increasingly diverse younger generations in the United States have turned to social media for information they trust, rejecting much of what traditional mainstream media have to say about them and their political and social aspirations (Freelon et al., 2018). These engaged citizen journalists do not wait around to be invited to join a website or download an app. They create many of their own practices and values. Among the ones identified here are (a) challenging the mainstream news media by offering alternative narratives and by confronting professional journalists; (b) outpacing the mainstream news media by operating faster, with more mobility and a willingness to stay with the story for long stretches of time; and (c) modeling new practices, both technologically and socially driven.

Claiming a right to their own narrative

Engaged citizen journalists often seek to offer a different narrative, one based on their own experiences, whether as members of a minority group going about their day-to-day lives before interrupted by some form of aggression or as witnesses or protesters demanding justice. One of their aims in producing media content is to challenge mainstream news narratives; this is accomplished in multiple ways.

One of the key ways the mainstream news accounts are challenged is by producing counter narratives. With social media platforms, citizen journalists can create and disseminate their own stories, originating from within their own communities. For example, when undocumented youth fought for their civil rights within the United States, they uploaded hundreds of personal videos telling their individual stories about why they are undocumented. They talked about how they saw themselves as Americans in what are labeled "coming out" videos that emphasize their humanity rather than through the commonly deployed lens of criminality (Jenkins, Shresthova, Gamber-Thompson, Kligler-Vilenchik, & Zimmerman, 2016). As one queer undocumented activist noted, "our stories are our weapons" (Lal, 2013, para. 5). As was reported in one typical video,

> My name is Cindy. I'm 21 years old. I'm undocumented. I'm unafraid. And I'm unapologetic. On March 10, 2011, we are going to have undocumented youth proclaim their undocumented status. They will tell everyone that they should not be sorry for being in the United States. That they should not apologize for getting an education, that they should not be sorry for their parents trying to make a living in the U.S.
>
> By coming out we share our stories. We put our face to this issue. We are human.
>
> (Hing, 2011, paras. 3–4)

These videos reporting undocumented people's own stories are important because research consistently shows that conflicts with the police, immigration officers and others by members of the public are often presented by mainstream news media from the point of view of the authorities, representing their actions as protecting the public through maintaining order (Hockin & Brunson, 2018; Willis & Painter, 2016). This is particularly so when the conflicts involve members of more marginalized groups, such as ethnic or religious minorities, immigrants and LGBTQ.

The pattern of police confrontations with community members over the shooting of unarmed African Americans follows this pattern (Araiza, Sturm, Istek, & Bock, 2016). Citizen journalists call out coverage that demonizes community members and echoes the administrative and police claims (Chen, 2014). This happens in part because professional journalists "have trouble crossing the social barriers that separated them from strangers" and much of the mainstream news media do not look like the victims of police violence (Araiza et al., 2016, p. 7). Even those who do come from ethnic or other marginalized groups are often also from elite classes and so also identify with those in power. In contrast, citizen journalists representing social movements often include in their content ordinary people who, when they appear in a mainstream news report, are often sliced and diced into neat soundbites or quotations paired with content from still other interviews from the "other side" in a he-said, she-said formula that muddies the facts to imply that victims of state violence deserve their treatment. In contrast, the engaged citizen journalist usually sides with the community perceived as under attack. This choice means the citizen reporter may be labeled "provocative" by the mainstream news, which works to keep citizen journalism at the margins of the field, particularly when it engages in coverage of racial justice–related issues (Araiza et al., 2016, p. 6). While some researchers, such as Freelon and colleagues (2018), argue that coverage of racial issues within the Twittersphere creates conditions in which citizen and profession journalism meet on more equal terrain, other studies find that when mainstream news media report using social media platforms, they repeat this pattern of support for the status quo (Barnard, 2018). In this way, engaged citizen journalists fill a gap in coverage.

Another way that engaged citizen journalism challenges the mainstream news is by pointing out what the latter get wrong or misunderstand. Amateur reporters may do so by providing evidence, such as video, that shows official claims are untrue: a person accused of resisting arrest may in fact be lying motionless on the ground. The affordances of social media platforms, such as Twitter, mean that corrections and challenges can be quickly and publicly posted and shared as well as added to through other eyewitness comments. These contributions of additional details by those responding to a post may lead to the correction of errors and the establishment of more accurate accounts of events. One of the more effective means of countering dominant frames is through the production of hashtags that give news narratives a different frame (Papacharisis, 2015). For example, young African Americans (and others) shared photos of themselves with their hands in the air, tagged #HandsUpDontShoot, as a means of emphasizing how innocent members of ethnic groups – even when they are submitting to the authorities by raising their hands in surrender – are targeted not for their actions but for their skin color in ways that can be lethal.

In some cases, citizens not only counter existing narratives but also create and disseminate their own. Freelon et al. (2018) found that Twitter is used by marginalized communities "to circulate and raise awareness about these concerns on their own terms without waiting for professional journalists to take interest" (p. 9). The U.S. police accountability movement called Cop Watch consists of grassroots groups of activists who follow the police, producing live streaming and other media content about their movements, which they believe will keep the officers in check. These self-appointed monitors often carry out their work in low-income neighborhoods where they believe the police may particularly feel emboldened to act with impunity. These citizen journalists differ from the "accidental journalists who happen upon beatings and shootings" (Bock, 2016, p. 14). Media scholar Mary Angela Bock (2016) argues that in carrying out this citizen surveillance work "the process of creating these narratives represent a form of active citizenship that gives voice to previously marginalized community concerns" (p. 14). Bock (2016) found that the cop watchers were sometimes confrontational with the police and that they "talked about themselves in terms of activism and not journalism" (p. 16).

Other witnesses (and victims) of individual acts of aggression are using a form of citizen journalism to reveal the sort of everyday discrimination African Americans and other ethnic minorities regularly face in ongoing attempts to police which public spaces they may use, regardless of their legal rights and civil liberties to do so (Anderson, 2015). This was particularly true in the summer of 2018 when a series of events produced witness videos, which went viral particularly when they were turned into memes complete with catchy nicknames for the perpetrators of white aggression. For example, a white woman (nickname: "BBQ Becky") told a group of African Americans that they could not barbecue in a public park near San Francisco because the rules forbid it; another white woman (nickname: "Pool Patrol Paula") in Summerville, South Carolina, slapped and insulted an African American youth who was part of a group of young people trying to swim in a community pool because she thought he "didn't belong" (O'Kane, 2018, para. 2). These events involved private accounts of oppression in public spaces that would likely never make it into a news report because such micro-acts of discrimination may not be taken seriously by the dominant white culture. Their documentation, sharing and likely the meme-making nicknames in fact brought these stories to national attention.

Challenging the mainstream news media

Another means for engaged citizen journalists to claim a space within public information streams has been to verbally and/or physically antagonize mainstream news media. In such cases, some citizen journalists publicly articulate a strong distrust and even disdain for professional news media and their practices. Among the most vocal critics are often the live streamers, who have taken on the role of some of the original bloggers from the early twenty-first century who monitored, criticized and "fisked" (fact-checked) the professionals. Writing about this new iteration of adversarial citizen journalists, Chen (2014, para. 2) says they sometimes view the mainstream as the "interlopers" on their turf. This behavior was seen with live streamers whose confrontations are purposefully carried out on camera so they can be viewed online as they happen. At the Ferguson protests, certain live streamers would spot reporters from mainstream news outlets, particularly from television, which is more identifiable because of their equipment, and try to provoke them in heated exchanges.

In one intense interaction, live streamer Jon Ziegler approached the KCTV5 (Kansas City) television news crew. Their reporter, Josh Marshall, had picked up a rock, looked into the camera and intoned that protesters at Ferguson were "throwing anything they could get their hands on" (Chen, 2014, para. 22). Ziegler became angry and confronted the KCTV5 reporter:

> "We're out here fucking 24 hours a day shooting live video that's unedited," Ziegler said in reply. "We sacrifice our lives. We sacrifice our safety to make sure that the lies the police spin and that you take and report as fact – because it's the police and they must not be lying – we are here to counter that narrative. And you just eat it up. And when you're not doing that, you just make it about yourself."
>
> (Chen, 2014, para. 29)

In another widely viewed video of an on-air confrontation, live streamer Bassem Masri shouts at and taunts CNN reporter Sara Sidner one night in Ferguson as she is covering the protests. Sidner is on her phone as Masri begins shouting, "Fake media's not allowed in Ferguson. Fake media's gotta go. We're holding y'all accountable . . . y'all keep lying we're gonna shut y'all down in Atlanta too" (Stelter, 2014).

Outpacing the MSM

Engaged citizen journalism that is focused in particular on political or crisis events has been marked by its speed, as its creators often post content faster than mainstream news media, which can be slowed down by usage of labor-intensive equipment and adherence to professional practices, such as confirming facts with multiple sources, or the desire for a more highly polished news product, particularly with regard to visual elements. In the case of the Ferguson protests, Araiza et al. (2016) found that due to their practices of posting high-quality images, professional news workers were sometimes "far from the action" when uploading content and thus produced work that was less compelling than visuals captured by citizen journalists who were physically in the middle of the most intense action.

Engaged citizen journalists often outpace the mainstream news in terms of being much more mobile (Araiza et al., 2016). Indeed, they often move with the protesters, blending in and adapting their movements to those of the demonstrators (Thorburn, 2014). In one iteration of this model, citizen journalists covering a student-fees protest movement in Quebec formed teams to intentionally mirror the fluidity of the protesters and used a spotter to identify potential footage in the crowds.

Many live streamers carry out marathon live broadcasting with hour-upon-hour of live footage. This commitment to coverage also allows them to embed with protesters and earn their trust as well as perhaps catch a unique flashpoint that the mainstream news misses. In Ferguson, Araiza et al. (2016) found some journalists trying to match the citizen journalist's speed. The researchers dubbed them "storm chasers" because their methods replicate professional news coverage of natural disasters. In Standing Rock, citizen journalists had to travel great distances to reach the encampment of the activists and, depending on which months they visited, endure extreme weather to cover the standoff with authorities over the pipeline. The commitment to staying in the field reflected a sort of ethnographic level of stamina for staying with the story. The downside is that constant connection with the story can produce burnout – in fact, sometimes quite rapidly. Jackson and Welles (2016, p. 39) found that some of these first-on-the-scene citizen reporters are "initiators" who provide heavy early coverage, creating a frame for the news in the first 24 hours of a conflict, and then quickly fade away, often to significantly slow down their posts or perhaps to never post about the conflict again.

Developing new practices

Seeking a different route to tell their stories, some engaged citizen journalists deploy new practices or techniques in their reporting. This conforms with studies of professional newsrooms that have found that citizen journalism or amateur practices in general, if considered effective, may be incorporated by mainstream news journalists into their own toolbox of techniques (Robinson & DeShano, 2011).

Citizen reporters, unbound by professional socialization, may create new practices simply because they have not been limited in how they view the possibilities of coverage. In some cases, they may become the inspiration or model for traditional journalists who begin to adopt their practices (Deluca & Lawson, 2014; Wall, 2015). Araiza et al. (2016) found mainstream journalists began to use the video app Vine after Ferguson alderman and citizen journalist Antonio French did so first and generated large audiences; they labeled him an "inspiration" (p. 6). Shadi Rahimi (2015) of AJ+ also adopted the citizen journalists' techniques, becoming with her reporting partner Brooke Minter the only professional team to use only their cell phones to report: "Much like activists and live streamers, when in Ferguson we live streamed, filmed and edited on our phones and tweeted photos and video as news broke" (para. 2). Just like the citizen live streamers, they worked continually, producing so much content their producers asked them to slow down. "We watched our audience grow as we scooped other news outlets on Twitter. No others were reporting this way. In the spaces between the breaking stories, we found ways to report more creatively for our social media audience" (Rahimi, 2015, para. 11).

News coverage on social media can be shallow and fail to convey in-depth information in part due to the features of the platforms. Yet, some citizen journalists, at least in the racial justice sphere, have sought to provide more in-depth information in innovative ways. Using social media, they contextualize what's happening by linking current events to related historical situations. In this way, they "create a long, thematic thread of narrative that links similar human rights violent actions to one another" (Richardson, 2017, p. 5). An example from Black Twitter is the rapid response to a white supremacist murdering nine churchgoers in Charleston, South Carolina. The #blacktwitter historians working with others created #CharlestonSyllabus, a collective endeavor to provide resources for those, including journalists, to educate the "public about the racial, economic, social and political underpinnings of breaking news events while reporters are still working to piece together timely elements of their story" (Clark, 2018, pp. 40–41). The creator of the syllabus said in an interview, "We started tweeting out suggested readings using the hashtag #CharlestonSyllabus. To my great surprise and pleasure, additional recommendations began pouring in. Within an hour, #CharlestonSyllabus was trending" (Williams, 2015, para. 5). This is counter-intuitive to our expectations about the abbreviated content that social media usually provides.

Fostering relationships

Citizen journalists in the midst of social and political conflicts are often highly responsive to and aware of their followers' expectations; in seeking to meet these, they model ways to maintain strong connections with audiences. As Chen (2014) points out, most of the live streamers covering Ferguson depended on crowd-funding in order to provide coverage, asking for financial support on sites such as Indiegogo and Fundrazr. These close connections mean that "their audience functions as a sort of crowd-sourced production team and assignment editor. Viewers offer tips about police and protester movement and help moderate the chat fields embedded in the feeds" (Chen, 2014, para. 11). Barnard's (2018) research found that citizen journalists were more likely than professional journalists to engage others on Twitter during the Ferguson demonstrations, participating in conversations and listening to others. In some cases, they were connected to larger networks with stronger ties than professional journalists were (Barnard, 2018).

The engaged citizen journalists also model new ways to connect with audiences in part through the affordances of technologies such as live streaming. Live streams have been shown to establish closer relationships with audiences through promoting live interactions and thus "higher intensity engagement" than other forms of video (Martini, 2018, p. 11). In general, live streaming prompts greater engagement through "immersion, immediacy, interaction, and sociality" (Haimson & Tang, 2017, p. 48). Importantly, live video can be experienced as a group even among those who are not co-present. "Live streams can make shared event experiences especially vivid by intertwining physical and digital experiences . . . [viewers experience a] shared sense of space and time that bridges the gap between event participants and audience" (Haimson & Tang, 2017, p. 50). These relationships are also seen as protecting members of the community by sharing with audiences what is happening, especially when police and other security services are using force against unarmed people. Live streams in particular provide visibility with the intention that authorities know what they are doing is being viewed by online audiences outside the space where their actions take place. Also, video streams have become evidence for legal defenses (Bock, 2016). A young protester was attacked by "alleged white supremacists" at the Unite the Right rally in Charlottesville, Virginia, and then was accused himself of beating the chairman of the North Carolina white nationalist group League of the South. The lawyers for the young protester used a citizen journalist's video to exonerate him (Williamson, 2018).

Related to this dynamic are the tone and approach that engaged citizen journalists may take; they are considered to be less subjective but also more emotional in the language and perspectives they use on social media. In fact, the aim, such as with the "Dreamers Coming Out" videos, is to connect emotionally with those who view the videos so as to humanize the undocumented and to gain support for their cause. While this may sometimes set amateurs apart from professionals, Barnard (2018) found that mainstream news journalists on Twitter also became more emotional when covering events such as Ferguson in part because they shared a mediated space and similar experiences with the protesters.

Conclusion

We know that engaged citizen journalism may provide an alternative narrative, particularly when it involves contentious political and social issues. What is of particular note here is that these more activist-oriented engaged citizen journalists are not trying to play by the mainstream news rules and they appear less concerned than previous generations of activist news producers that they be amplified by professional reporters. Instead, they are creating news ecologies of their own, producing their own streams of news and information (Wall, 2018). This information is attractive to others because the engaged citizen journalist can provide content unavailable elsewhere; it can help meet a seemingly insatiable desire for ongoing streams of information particularly during times of intense conflict. It can introduce unexpected views. For example, live streamer Bassem Masri (2014) offered audiences different insights on Ferguson when he pointed out that the police actions such as stop and frisk and use of military weapons and tactics against civilians reminded him of the ways the Israeli military operated in his homeland of Palestine. Such comments may be difficult to find elsewhere.

Are these strengths also weaknesses? Ubiquity of content appears to go hand in hand with the lack of a coherent story. A list of live streamers at Standing Rock numbered 31 and ranged from Lakota activist Ladonna Brave Bull Allard to a live stream created by a water protector's encampment, Oceti Sakowin Camp. While this suggests a bounty of views, it also can make complicated issues more difficult to decipher for those not closely following due to the large amount of citizen-produced coverage (DeLuca & Lawson, 2014). Engaged citizen journalism can be about capturing the emotion of the moment and, while sometimes those emotions may foster a shared humanity, such as with the Dreamers, in other cases, they may express frustration and anger. Such feelings might be directed at the structures that oppress people or they may simply bubble up and explode in unpredictable and even harmful moments.

3 Enraged citizen journalism

In the summer of 2009, conservative activist and self-described citizen journalist James O'Keefe and a confederate, Hannah Giles, approached various
offices of ACORN, the 40-year-old Association of Community Organizations for Reform Now (ACORN), which advocated for voter rights, health
care and access to housing for low-income Americans. O'Keefe and Giles
carried out "sting" operations against ACORN, visiting its offices in Balti-
more, Philadelphia, New York, Los Angeles and other locations, secretly
filming their visits. In selectively edited videos, the pair tells ACORN
employees that they want the organization's help in avoiding paying taxes
for a proposed prostitution business. Some of the organization's workers
appeared to try to advise them on how to carry this action out. The videos were further enhanced by inserting video of O'Keefe walking near the
offices wearing a fur chinchilla coat and sunglasses while holding a cane,
to appear as what he thought a pimp would look like. He actually did not
wear this outfit in the office visits but edited the video to appear that he did.

He took his edited videos to right-wing media figure Andrew Breitbart,
who described them as "the Abu Ghraib of the Great Society" and pro-
ceeded to help O'Keefe develop a plan to release them to greatest effect
(Lewis, 2009, para 14). Other conservative media, such as Fox News' Sean
Hannity, followed, gleefully amplifying the videos as evidence of the cor-
ruption of the organization. Despite ACORN's protests that the videos were
out of context and failed to include employees informing police about the
visits, a political firestorm erupted. The videos resulted in the U.S. Congress
eliminating its funding for ACORN and, more damaging to the organization, its main funders stopped giving it money (Beam, 2010; Acorn and the
Firestorm, 2018). In California, because O'Keefe had recorded ACORN
employees without their knowledge, he was in violation of state law. Then
Attorney General Jerry Brown's office granted O'Keefe and Giles immu-
nity in exchange for publicly releasing the tapes. A California ACORN

employee, who had reported O'Keefe to the police, won a $100,000 lawsuit against him (Ungar, 2013).

O'Keefe embodies enraged citizen journalism, a form that works to activate those who thrive on conflict and may exhibit little concern for ethical norms of professional journalism or even the truth. While much of what is written about citizen journalism emphasizes it as a positive development, scholars such as Al-Ghazzi (2014) suggest one may take up the mantle of citizen journalism in the name of more insidious and propagandistic goals. Such uses can include encouraging physical violence or simply modeling hateful rhetoric. This line of thought argues that our misunderstanding of the modern forms of digital citizen journalism was clear in the case of the Middle East Arab Spring, which has been presented as a key example of the widespread view that citizen journalism is the means to "mobilize political action against brutal dictatorships" (Al-Ghazzi, 2014, p. 436). In reality, though, citizen journalism has been just as likely to be "used as a weapon of war and tool of torture" (Al-Ghazzi, 2014, p. 436). These more disturbing variants are not limited to any particular regions or associated only with low-income or highly authoritarian countries. As U.S. media watchdog Media Matters proclaimed about the political process in the United States, "The 2016 election emboldened dangerous 'citizen journalist' vigilantes" who abetted the dissemination of disinformation and the rise of conspiracy theories on social media platforms that literally inspired threats against people's lives ("The 2016 election," 2016). We forget this at our peril. As Mano (2010) warns, these "emerging new media spaces function like double-edged swords able to either build or destroy democracy" (p. 57).

Enraged citizen journalism

An alternative genealogy of citizen journalism in the United States offers a related yet darker iteration of the phenomenon highlighted in Chapter 2. This family tree starts with the rise of right-wing political news maestro Matt Drudge, now considered one of the most influential agenda setters and amplifiers in the conservative news media world, and continues with his alt-right heirs, such as Andrew Breitbart, founder of *Breitbart News*, Alex Jones, founder of *InfoWars*, and James O'Keefe, founder of Project Veritas, and a multitude of other, lesser-known progeny who have proclaimed themselves part of a "citizen journalism movement" (O'Keefe, 2013, p. 334). As Andrew Breitbart proclaimed at a Tea Party rally on the Washington, D.C., mall, "We are a citizen journalism army, and we are going to take this country back" (Hohmann, 2010, para. 4).

Despite criticisms that these members of the so-called alt-right news sphere engage in unethical practices and are often focused on misinformation and propaganda, their work appeals to millions of people who prefer such content, often rejecting traditional conservative news sites in favor of inflammatory content that can be racist, misogynist and anti-immigrant (Bhat, 2018; Faris et al., 2017; Durham, 2018; Lakshmanan, 2017). *Infowars*, hosted by Alex Jones, who claims the Sandy Hook elementary school shootings in which 20 children and six adults were murdered was a hoax, airs on 129 radio stations; Jones also is said to generate more than 80 million video views in a single month (Roig-Franzia, 2016). Many alt-right media producers create starkly different versions of reality than mainstream news media, constructed in part by reimagining journalism through their own interpretations of its practices. Many embody the early 2000s blogger's rage against the mainstream news media. In doing so, they often demonstrate "flagrant disregard for the conventional norms of news reporting" (Allan, 2006, p. 43). Some might argue that they are not actually journalism.

While little commented upon, it turns out these hyper-partisan media makers embrace the term "citizen journalism" even as its use has declined as the term of choice for many American journalists, who have moved on to more specific designations, such as participatory, crowd-sourced, witnessing and other labels for variations of amateur-produced journalism. Indeed, this chapter argues that the term "citizen journalism" has become part of the identity of many alt-right content creators, and a moniker they commonly use when they talk about their work. In their views of themselves, they are pugnacious, determined voices, willing to "take on the powers that be" (Lee, 2015, para. 12), as they pursue a simple aim: to "try to get to the bottom of the truth" (Marx, 2010, para. 4). In doing so, they seek to differentiate themselves from traditional, professional journalists – even some of those on the right – and the use of the citizen journalist label appears to be part of their strategy. While the public identity they offer for themselves would appear to align them with the citizen journalists agitating against the system in Chapter 2, in fact they are not merely the other side of the same coin. These enraged citizen journalists are more oriented toward hyping the populist grievances primarily of whites rather than restoring basic rights to all people, such as to vote and be safe in their interactions with police. These interlopers storming the gates of mainstream news often "run roughshod over relatively established notions of liberalism and societal normalcy" (Eldridge, 2018, p. 5).

This chapter begins by tracing the origins of this enraged citizen journalism to the rise in the 1990s of blogger Matt Drudge, seen today as a godfather of right-wing citizen journalism. It teases out their practices as they have evolved over the last two decades. Other key figures in this movement are highlighted, followed by consideration of the ways enraged citizen journalism comes into being through a particular staging or performance of journalism.

Paternity test: Matt Drudge, a citizen journalism forefather

The rise of the right-wing news sphere has been tied to the muckraking traditions from British pamphleteers to the early twentieth-century journalist I. F. Stone (Sambrook, 2009). Its modern-day heirs are said to work in a new genre of journalism, often practiced as a digital form of "tabloidism" or even vigilante journalism (Scott, 2007, p. 54). Much of this sphere of activity can be traced to one-time blogger Matt Drudge, today's impresario of the conservative news ecosystem. In the mid-1990s, when journalism was being reinvented in a digital world, Drudge was working as a runner at a CBS Television gift shop but harboring aspirations for the future from his Hollywood apartment. He was soon to launch his own digital publication, the *Drudge Report*, a sometimes incendiary and rule-breaking website, consisting mainly of a collection of links to other sites, taking a "shortcut through journalism standards" as he was driven by sense of what would attract audiences (Scott, 2007, p. 53).

In the swirl of leaks, tips and "salacious gossip" that frequently featured on the site, Drudge broke through to large-scale public attention in part by pursuing one particularly compelling story: U.S. president Bill Clinton's affair with White House intern Monica Lewinsky (Allan, 2006). "[C]ombining the sensibilities of a gadfly, a seemingly unquenchable hunger for celebrity, acceptance, and power," Drudge would print details and speculation that mainstream news would not; ultimately, however, the professionals believed themselves forced to compete on his terms in an attempt to maintain control of the story (Williams & Delli Carpini, 2000, p. 72). In trying to protect its boundaries by placing Drudge outside of them but mimicking his work, the mainstream news media ended up rejecting its own values. While assimilating newcomers might traditionally work as a means of neutralizing their threat to a field, here, the profession itself was changed in the process, as the rise of Drudge ultimately "undermin[ed] the commonsense assumptions used by both elites, citizens and scholars to understand the role of the media in a democratic society" (Williams & Delli Carpini, 2000, p. 62).

Drudge went on to have enormous impact on journalism, particularly as practiced on the right. What is of particular interest in this chapter is how the right-wing news sphere viewed his work. Andrew Breitbart (2011, p. 149) declared in his writings about the inspirational model the *Drudge Report* created for himself and others: "Drudge was a citizen journalist." Drudge himself echoed that description, emphasizing that amateur muckrakers in the future would potentially include everyone: "We have entered an era vibrating with the din of small voices. Every citizen can be a reporter, can take on the powers that be" (Lee, 2015, para. 12). Such claims were not unusual from all sides of the political spectrum in the early days of citizen journalism. Amateurs would overcome the failings of traditional, mainstream professional journalism, and new information spheres would be formed by citizen journalists seeking to work outside the traditional system. Observers on the right glowingly described sites such as *Breitbart News* as performing a public service as they were "dedicated to more voices, not less" (NavigationArts Next Generation Web Design, 2012, para. 3).

In carrying out enraged citizen journalism, its practitioners are willing not only to report but also to create the news. They reject many accepted practices, often operating as if they don't exist. It is not uncommon for these right-wing citizen journalists to want to rid society of what they consider professional journalism entirely (with the exception of Fox News). Their attitude is seen in their chosen metaphors that evoke a battleground for their particularly aggressive vision of what they see as grassroots journalism. Hence, alt-right citizen journalists are "happy warriors" (Balek, 2015) and "insurgents" or, as James O'Keefe (2013) called his Project Veritas reporters, "the Green Berets of citizen journalism" (p. 5).

Yet the citizen journalism that has been embraced by the right wing is quite a bit different from the engaged citizen journalist. While it might be argued that the racial justice–seeking citizen journalists who shout at mainstream reporters are the same as the right-wing ones, the aims are different – for example, in terms of seeking to retain legal rights versus trying to take them away from others. Black Twitter denizens, for instance, are oftentimes resisting oppression, not trying to suppress others. Engaged citizen reporters document the racial bias and violence toward communities of color by the police (and other institutions). That community's safety – indeed, its members' very lives – can be at stake. Nearly all of these white male conservative citizen journalists seek to limit others' rights, whether they are African Americans seeking to vote or Muslims hoping for a voice in the public sphere.

Rise of the alt-right version of citizen journalism

Others followed in Drudge's footsteps, often with an assist from the influential blogger. A key example is Breitbart, who worked for Drudge for nearly a decade as a second-in-command (Beam, 2010). From there, he joined Ariana Huffington, Jonah Peretti (later co-founder of Buzzfeed) and Kenneth Lerer (a former AOL executive) as a co-founder of the *Huffington Post*, which was initially envisioned as a citizen journalism-type site. Breitbart had previously worked as a researcher for Huffington when she was a conservative, but she was a liberal when she hired him and he lasted only three weeks after the site's launch. He left to start his own series of conservative blogs, such as *Big Government, Big Hollywood* and, in 2005, *Breitbart News*, that would reflect his own vision for these new digital news forms. Described as a "hyper-partisan" "media insurgent" who "reverted to pre-professional practices of American journalism," he proclaimed that his sites were based on the principles of citizen journalism (Bhat, 2018, pp. 192, 200; Durham, 2018, p. 188; NavigationArts Next-Generation Web Design Continues Andrew Breitbart's Vision, 2012). As Breitbart told Fox News commentator Sean Hannity, "It is a citizen journalism revolution that's going on right now and I'm trying to be the pied piper to show you how" (Hannity, 2011, para. 7). Just as Drudge created his version of journalism, so Breitbart did not bother to imitate established conservative news media. Instead, his site embodied the confrontational tone characteristic of the Tea Party movement and talk radio: hyperbolic and aggressive. Breitbart became a hero to the alt-right and a villain to liberals who called him a "rightwing jihadist" (Durham, 2018, p. 188). He rejected any appearance of even-handedness and exaggerated already inflammatory conventional conservative reporting, producing a site in which "invectives and hate" fueled much of his content (Eldridge, 2018, p. 169). It would attack "Republican elites, foster anti-immigrant sentiment and promote political conspiracy theories" (Bhat, 2018, p. 197). He also continued to describe his work as citizen journalism, a description widely accepted and lauded in the right-wing information sphere. Breitbart wrote in his book, *Righteous Indignation: Excuse Me While I Save the World*, that "at my websites I wanted to supply a . . . platform for citizen journalists" (Breitbart, 2011, p. 222).

Sites such as this would claim that they were able to report the truth because they are not constrained by traditional journalism practices and that embracing citizen journalism was part of that. "Breitbart, lacking the reservations of mainstream outlets to promote citizen journalism, was able to dominate the news cycle in innovative ways" (Bloom, 2012, para. 4). He "showed people what they could do with their stories" (Hartog, 2012, para. 25). This sometimes meant passing along unverified or unsavory content promoting "race-based nationalism and white superiority" (Bhat, 2018, p. 197). Indeed, Eldridge (2018) noted that Breitbart's "content ranges from willfully misleading . . . to outright hate-filled" as it thrives on "disinformation" (p. 171).

After Breitbart died of a heart attack, provocateur Steve Bannon took over *Breitbart News*, using the site to support the presidential campaign of the man who would become president: Donald Trump. In analyzing the 2016 U.S. presidential election, Harvard researchers noted that the old conservative media were losing their audiences and influence: "The rising prominence of Breitbart along with relatively new outlets such as the Daily Caller marks a significant reshaping of the conservative media landscape" (Faris et al., 2017, p. 11). Sites such as *InfoWars* became "key touchstones in the Trump media sphere, offering up a range of conspiracy theories, thinly veiled racism and xenophobia, and rampant misinformation" (Faris et al., 2017, p. 44). In public remarks and on their own sites, these leaders of the alt-right media sphere continued to describe themselves as enabling citizen journalists. Yet the sites themselves do not offer obvious citizen journalism entry points as seen in traditional news media sites.

When mainstream media outlets solicit citizen content, they usually offer transparent directions for how to submit, such as a "share your videos here." Despite claims of solidarity with citizen journalism, there is little evidence that *Breitbart News* provides for that kind of participation, which would be open to anyone to have their work appear on his site. Likewise, *InfoWars* merely allows call-ins to its radio show. Breitbart suggested that merely retweeting would be an act of citizen journalism: "Using my ubiquity rule, the citizen journalist isn't always reporting the ledes, headlines and paragraphs forms" (Breitbart, 2011, p. 156). Thus, it appears much of its citizen participation comes from pulling "information" from social media and amplifying it as well as occasionally hosting the people producing such content. One such individual who initially described himself as a citizen journalist was Mike Cernovich, whom the Southern Poverty Law Center, which tracks hate groups around the United States, describes as "acting as a pass-through for thinly-sourced and conspiratorial scoops" (Making News Through Trolling, n.d., para. 2).

Despite their emphasis on citizen journalism, connections with one outlet in right-wing corporate media were strong. Millionaire pundits on Fox News, such as Sean Hannity, consistently promoted some of these conservative citizen reporters. Likewise, while projecting an image of being connected to the grassroots, Breitbart was actually funded not just by advertising but also by billionaire hedge fund manager Robert Mercer, credited with creating an "alternative media ecosystem" (Bhat, 2018; Gold, 2017, para. 3). The connections with the powerful are further seen in the creation of the Andrew Breitbart Award for Citizen Journalism by the highly influential conservative think tank the Heritage Foundation, which partnered with the Franklin Center to create the accolade.

Of his own mastery of what he calls citizen journalism, James O'Keefe said that he learned it could be practiced "without a degree or pedigree" (Lee, 2012, para. 5). As noted earlier, this overlaps with general non-ideological claims about citizen journalism: "every citizen can be a reporter" (Lee, 2012, para. 5). As O'Keefe (2013) notes, his vision of the citizen journalist was not something offered by a mainstream news media app but rather an identity a person selected for him or herself. In his memoir, *Breakthrough: Our Guerilla War to Expose Fraud and Save Democracy*, he called his work "my self-created career as a citizen journalist" (O'Keefe, 2013, p. 5). Interestingly, he defined his work as a "career," when citizen journalism is generally considered to be unpaid volunteer contributions.

In his second book, *American Pravda: My Fight for Truth in an Era of Fake News*, O'Keefe (2013, 2018) continues to describe himself as a citizen journalist, envisioning that role as a form of investigative journalism among other things. O'Keefe describes it this way: "We used the same tactics that investigative journalists have been using. In all the videos I do, I pose as something I'm not to try to get to the bottom of the truth" (Marx, 2010, para. 3). But in his enactment of citizen journalism, the pursuit of the story trumps other considerations and thus secret cameras, disguises and other forms of deceit are part of his toolkit, as evidenced in his ACORN pieces. He does not see himself crossing ethical lines but instead as an object of hate and derision because of "powerful forces aligned, fairly or not, against the citizen journalist" (O'Keefe, 2013, p. 157). It is his effectiveness, he believes, that leads the mainstream news media and other elites to "curse the citizen journalist" (O'Keefe, 2013, p. 175).

Founding an organization called Project Veritas, he said "we are equipping citizen journalists to go out . . . and investigate" (O'Keefe, 2013, p. 165). More recently he focused the organization on shadowing and secretly filming mainstream journalists in ways that would damage their news organizations, such as when he pretended be a potential donor to the National Public Radio Foundation and recorded its executive who was meeting with him saying negative things about Republicans. The end result was the foundation executive and NPR's CEO Vivian Schiller being forced to resign. In his project called "To Catch a Journalist," Project Veritas offers large "rewards" for undercover infiltration and filming of news organizations: "as part of an effort to take down the media through citizen journalism. If you have hidden audio recordings, videotapes or documents inside of a newsroom or media institution, and the material is good enough, I will pay you $10,000" (Kew, 2017, para. 1). While O'Keefe writes a great deal about his independence and challenges to the status quo, he still wants to influence the traditional mainstream news media. "You have to get covered by the mainstream media," O'Keefe told a group of college students in Chicago. "That's what success is" (Svitek, 2013, para. 9).

Performing citizen journalism

Meet our citizen journalists, proclaims the host of the television show *The Opposition w/ Jordan Klepper* as the camera cuts away to wacky people reporting from their own basements and rallies for President Trump. In this episode of the show, "citizen reporter" Kobi Libii visits Twin Falls, Idaho, where a Syrian refugee is alleged to have raped a 5-year-old girl. Libii tells the audience, "Muslim refugees are dangerous. I know because I've never met one." *The Opposition* is not actually another conspiracy theory site, but instead a parody television show about such media launched in the fall of 2017 by Comedy Central.

The show embodies the argument by Eldridge (2018) that in some ways certain actors within the right-wing media sphere are performing journalism or at least attempting to. Describing these citizen journalists as engaged in performance does not mean they have no effect or that they are only entertainment (although for some, they will be). These performances are a means of engaging their audiences to accept and take pleasure in their mendacity by triggering an emotional connection to the content. As a researcher from the online fact checking site Snopes noted about conspiracy theories, they are "supposed to be emotional, make you angry" (Palma, 2018). None of which is meant to make light of what such sites are doing. As Johnson (2018) argues, conspiracy theory discourse can radicalize its audiences, most of whom are white men.

At the beginning of every episode of *The Opposition*, Klepper stands in front of a stereotypical conspiracy theorist's bulletin board, peppered with "news clippings from the 'fake news' media, connected by literal stray threads" to illustrate the ways its practitioners sometimes seek to make illogical connections (Framke, 2017, para. 16). In this episode, Libii attends the Citizen Journalism School taught by Breitbart reporter Lee Stranahan (who was referenced in the Department of Justice's investigation of President Trump's presidential campaign's possible conspiracy with the Russian government). By the end of the episode, *The Opposition*'s fake citizen journalist finds that the story he is investigating is itself fake.

This idea that citizen journalism is also a performance shouldn't be a surprise. Consider Matt Drudge's entry onto the national media scene, in which he appeared during interviews wearing a fedora to harken back to earlier ages of journalism. He was not just aggregating salacious links; he was inventing a persona, which some likened to gossip columnist Walter Winchell, who more than a half century earlier married journalism to entertainment (Gabler, 1995). Indeed, conservatives such as O'Keefe describe what they do as more than reporting; they are, he argues, "guerilla journalists" who employ "culture jamming" as a key practice (O'Keefe, 2013, pp. 28, 83). A Slate profile of Andrew Breitbart noted that "He considers himself a journalist-slash-entertainer, an Edward R. Murrow by way of the Merry Pranksters" (Beam, 2010, para. 7).

James O'Keefe has variously likened himself to Tom Wolfe's maumauing the flak catchers or the political satirical actors the "Yes Men," whose techniques include impersonation and fake websites. O'Keefe has also described his work as having "elements of gonzo," "Borat" and "guerrilla theater" (O'Keefe, 2013, p. 188). Some observers from the mainstream news media agree that what he shows the world is "part new-media mogul, part Barnumesque scamp" (Oney, 2010, p. 35). In Alex Jones's custody case with his ex-wife, his lawyer argued that the *InfoWars* host is only playing a character (Rhodan, 2017). His defense attorney, Randall Wilhite, said during the pretrial hearing that Jones says what he does because "He is a performance artist" (Rhodan, 2017, para. 2). "Jonathan Tilove, an *American-Statesman* reporter covering the trial, tweeted that the lawyers described their client's on-air persona as having the ability to combine 'humor, bombasity, sarcasm, wit'" (Killelea, 2017, para. 4). Jones contradicted his own defense about his seriousness on his show and eventually lost the case.

As these right-wing provocateurs perform citizen journalism, they have taken over the label, converting it into a category to support their own ends as they produce identity more so than actual information (Kreiss, 2018). NPR's *On the Media* show asks, "What is O'Keefe, anyway? A prankster, an activist, a muckraker, a citizen journalist?" (What the Media Can Learn from James O'Keefe, 2011). This mixing of roles, which satirizes being a journalist, does not mean what they are doing is not real nor does it mean some if not all of them believe what that say. Nevertheless, at least some of their audiences believe it is news. The others are in on the joke. It is, in sum, "theatrics" for some and the hidden truth for others (Nazaryan, 2018, para. 8). By taking the title of citizen journalist, the actors are, of course, intentionally setting themselves apart from the mainstream news media and by turning what they do into performances, they are also drawing a bold line between themselves and those who produce traditional news. This conclusion led *Los Angeles Times* entertainment critic Patrick Goldstein (2011) to ask, "Why has the mainstream media treated O'Keefe's provocative pranks as major news stories? After all, when Ali G and Borat used almost exactly the same technique to embarrass people, it was treated as clever satire" (para. 13).

Meanwhile, their performance of citizen journalism continues apace. O'Keefe sent a plant to the *Washington Post* just before the 2017 U.S. Senate election in Alabama with a concocted story that she had been a victim of the Republican Senate candidate Roy Moore, who was under investigation for child molestation claims. The reporters did their due diligence and concluded that she was a fraud. They met with her, told her that and informed her they were filming her reactions. The additional attention also meant the funding for Project Veritas, which is registered as a 501(3)c non-profit, was highlighted by some news outlets. O'Keefe, who claims to be a sort of everyman, earned a salary of $320,000 and received a nearly $1.7 million donation in 2016 from a charity affiliated with archconservative billionaire industrialists Charles and David Koch (O'Harrow, 2017). He also accepted a $10,000 donation from the Trump Foundation and received an invitation to the 2017 inauguration of the forty-fifth president of the United States (Weigel, 2017).

Another outcome of the rise of these right-wing citizen journalists has been to inspire others to attempt to follow in their footsteps. One well-known example of how such unmoored reporting can have serious consequences was the way citizen reporters helped push the so-called #Pizzagate conspiracy theory. The theory was that U.S. presidential candidate Hillary Clinton and her political adviser, John Podesta, were running a pedophile ring in the basement of a popular restaurant, Comet Pizza, in Washington, D.C. A former Naval intelligence officer who has been identified as a "citizen journalist," Jack Posobiec, visited Comet Pizza to investigate the rumors and live streamed his time there (Fisher, Cox, & Hermann, 2016; McLaughlin, 2017; Sommer, 2018, para. 2). A Comet Pizza manager called the police after seeing Posobiec filming a children's birthday party at the restaurant, and police escorted him out. McLaughlin (2017) says Posobiec then appeared on *InfoWars*, describing his experience. Jones himself repeatedly talked about the made-up pedophile ring on *InfoWars*. Not long after, a North Carolina man drove to the restaurant, armed with a shotgun, a Colt .38 handgun and an AR-15 assault rifle, and began shooting into the establishment. He said in an interview he listened to *InfoWars*.

Conclusion

Vitriol attracts audiences, an attraction the algorithms and other structural features of social media are designed to enhance. In this way, the promise of the Arab Spring with citizen journalists using social media to call for greater freedoms has given way to darker scenarios around the world – from lies about pedophiles operating in a pizza restaurant in the capital city of the United States to equally false assertions that Muslims were trying to sterilize Buddhists in a small town in Sri Lanka. Both of these particular lies prompted acts of violence; in the latter, it was deadly. In countries like Sri Lanka with weaker institutions, citizens conveying news on such platforms can initiate riots, lynchings and even murder among communal groups (Taub & Fisher, 2018). This enraged form of citizen journalism may spread like a virus in the future, carrying stories of hate along with the incitement to act on those emotions.

4   Learning from other disciplines

Journalism is not the only discipline that has seen the rise of ordinary people taking part in the collection, analysis and sometimes creation of different forms of information and cultural content. Citizen participation may occur in examinations of the natural world, the enactment of art projects, humanitarian actions responding to disasters, the creation of historical archives and more. Indeed, a range of institutions and disciplines now solicit various forms of participation within their realms (D'Ignazio & Zuckerman, 2017). Some of these projects have been highly successful at generating involvement, such as the inclusion of millions of people playing a role in the implementation of citizen science projects. Such activities often include carrying out actions that are similar to journalism: the collection of original information through in-person or online observations and well as the assessment and analysis of data, whether self-collected or supplied online through massive databases. In other cases, citizens may collaborate in the collective production of creative content or performances, some of which might raise awareness or even enact responses to important social and political issues. As with journalism, the practices and aims of incorporating amateurs and various types of "in-betweeners" into these diverse disciplines are varied (Ahva, 2017, p. 1).

This chapter aims to contribute to our understanding of participatory practices in these disciplines in order to broaden our thinking about citizen journalism efforts. In particular, I focus on two arenas that have incorporated citizen participation into their work: science and the arts. Each arose from different histories and aims and, of course, different epistemological frameworks. It can be argued that journalism sits somewhere between the highly empirical discipline of science and the heavily interpretive practices of the arts. Driven by different goals and debates, these arenas can provide us with alternative lenses and vocabularies for thinking about citizen participation in the production of information and knowledge.

Citizen science

From collecting mosquitos (29,000 and counting) to scanning deep space for new stars, millions of amateurs have joined forces with professional scientists to increase our knowledge about scientific questions that may affect people's health, climate change and more. As a leading proponent of citizen science, Caren Cooper (2016) writes, "ordinary people are changing the face of discovery." Their activities fall under the category of citizen science, which has no single definition, although it has been described as "a diversity of techniques that engage the public in scientific investigation and science-based learning" (Phillips, Ferguson, Minarchek, Porticella, & Bonney, 2014, p. 1). Eitzel and colleagues (2017) offer the more succinct explanation: citizen science is "the inclusion of members of the public in some aspect of scientific research" (p. 5). Citizen scientists, then, are people who are taking part in collective scientific endeavors (Cooper, 2016). Citizen science as we know it today is traced to different origins; some connect it with the rise of Big Data and a need to enlist large numbers of volunteers to help manage enormous amounts of information, while others like to point out that citizen science has existed since at least the early twentieth century and perhaps much earlier as inspired amateurs sought to better understand the natural world through activities such as measuring tides or watching the stars (Cooper, 2016). Indeed, they argue science itself was the invention of ordinary but curious people.

Evidence of the rise of citizen science today is seen in its increasing visibility and growing popularity. For instance, well-known citizen science platform Zooniverse has 1.4 million registered users and more than 40 active citizen science projects in disciplines ranging from astrology to genetics (Masters et al., 2016). On the site, citizens participate in activities such as classifying "millions of images of galaxies, moon craters or sea-floor organisms" (Bonney et al., 2014, p. 1436). International and national citizen science organizations now include the European Citizen Science Association, the Australian Citizen Science Association and the world's largest, the U.S.-based Citizen Science Association, whose members come from 80 different countries. Beyond these organizations, uncountable numbers of unaffiliated grassroots citizen science projects are taking place around the globe as well (Eitzel et al., 2017). Citizen scientists have received awards from U.S. president Barack Obama and they even have an official day: April 14, Citizen Science Day. The U.S. city of Boulder, Colorado, prioritized citizen science in its city planning as part of its Resilience Strategy to meet the challenges of the future.

Purpose/aims

The aims of citizen science vary by project and initiator but tend to fall under several main categories:

- Aiding scientists in analyzing large data sets seen as too big to be handled solely by professionals. Eitzel and colleagues (2017) argue this is the "instrumental view," focused on achieving greater efficiency in carrying out the work of professional scientists. These are not merely empty exercises. For example, the work of citizen contributors to "Zooniverse projects ha[s] yielded more than 50 peer-reviewed articles on topics ranging from galaxies to oceans" (Bonney et al., 2014, p. 1436).
- Engaging ordinary people in an appreciation of science and scientific processes. "If we can enthuse our audience, they can and have become advocates for our projects" (Why Work Together, n.d., para. 2). Proponents of citizen science also articulate broader goals, believing that participation in citizen science projects encourages participants to become better stewards of the environment and fosters greater connections with the natural world. Participants will care more deeply about the natural environment and be more willing to support science and to value the protection of nature.
- Democratizing science in ways that separate it from its elitist tendencies. In particular, forms of citizen science that fall under categories such as community-based aim to "broaden participation in science, so we are essentially in the business of redefining or even disassembling boundaries" between professionals and communities (Eitzel et al., 2017, p. 4). Some scientists even consider citizen science to be a "form of resistance" as it offers a counter view to elite science, intentionally locating itself at the "peripheries" of the field (Eitzel et al., 2017, p. 9). As science becomes increasingly complex and difficult for ordinary people to grasp, the role of citizen science in making at least some aspects of it more accessible and understandable to the public can "restore public trust in science" and be more inclusive (Eitzel et al., 2017, p. 7). This will become increasingly important as the public's understanding cannot keep up with advances and may be subject to misinformation by powerful forces in society or they will somehow be incorporated as "participants" without direct permission.

Forms of participation

As with citizen journalism, the forms and aims of participation are debated within citizen science. Haklay (2012) categorizes citizen science by the intensity of the activity, suggesting that "basic" participation involves citizens as sensors and simple "interpreters," such as when they are tagging or categorizing data or perhaps simply allowing their idle computer to remotely help process large-scale data sets (p. 166). In higher-level forms of participation, citizens help to identify the research problem to be pursued and help collect data. The highest level finds citizens collaborating with scientists in the co-production of professional research. Still other scientists suggest the following categories to characterize participation: (a) contributory, where a citizen scientist's activities are "observation, identification and monitoring" data; (b) collaborative, in which citizen scientists develop explanations and design projects; (c) co-creative, in which the citizen scientist helps define research questions, carry out the research, and interpret and disseminate results (Becker-Klein, Peterman, & Stylinski, 2016, p. 8).

As with citizen journalism, observers suggest that with the rise of digital media, crowd sourcing and related activities that can be achieved online have come to dominate many forms of participation emphasized in citizen science (Literat, 2016). Not as frequent but still common are citizen science data collection projects that require in-person participation, such as the birders from around the world who have been recruited by the Cornell Lab of Ornithology to collect data in real-world spaces, providing "more than five million bird observations every month" (Bonney, et al., 2014, p. 1436). In another example, the U.S. National Park Service brought together citizens for the Los Angeles Urban Coyote Project to set up and run wildlife cameras in green spaces and residential yards, to report sightings to the iNaturalist site as well as to sift through coyote scat to help determine what the animals were eating in urban environments. Such participation is not merely engaging citizens with the natural world: the data being collected matters to researchers. Cooper, Shirk and Zuckerberg (2014) found that more than half of the studies of the impact of climate change on aviation migration patterns they evaluated "depended on data from citizen scientists" (p. 3). In fact, they and other scientists are calling for recognition of citizen scientists' contributions, be it through acknowledgments in a paper's footnotes for minor contributions or, in the case of major contributions, being listed as co-authors.

Evaluation

Citizen science projects frequently undergo various forms of evaluation. In various parts of the Western world, such projects are financially supported by university programs or other entities, such as natural history or other science-related museums or research centers (Eitzel et al., 2017). These institutional supporters commonly require measurable evidence of levels of involvement and impact on attitudes or behaviors of participants as a condition of providing funding and/or renewing grants. Likewise, because citizen science has been closely tied to science education in places such as American public schools, projects may need to meet their requirements for demonstrating impact through various methods of assessment. Dickinson and colleagues (2012) find that common indicators for success include participation, knowledge gains and understanding of scientific processes.

There is a growing infrastructure to support the fostering of common norms and evaluation of them for citizen science. One example is the launch of an academic journal specifically focused on the phenomenon: *Citizen Science: Theory and Practice*. Here the field can be debated as well as researched in peer-reviewed articles. Other public arenas include citizen science conferences at which techniques and strategies for implementing projects take center stage. Indeed, the second biannual Citizen Science Association Conference held in 2017 in Minnesota attracted more than 1,000 delegates (Roche & Davis, 2017). This attention to measuring impact is further evident in the development of specific tools for assessing outcomes. Among these are the W.K. Kellogg Foundation's "citizen science logic model," which generates a formula for tracking and measuring the accomplishments of participatory science projects (Phillips, Bonney, & Shirk, 2012, p. 93).

Because much citizen science participation is online, researchers aiming to assess citizen participation often analyze that data to try to identify changes in behaviors and/or attitudes or to track evidence of knowledge increase about a specific topic (Phillips et al., 2012). For example, Masters et al. (2016) looked for changes in the vocabulary of participants in Zooniverse projects to indicate knowledge gains. Others measure levels of engagement. Cornell Lab of Ornithology's Nestwatch project assesses the online communications of citizen scientists working on their project to see how frequently participants share data and how often they participate in discussions with each other (Phillips et al., 2012). Similar to citizen journalism, there are debates concerning the quality of the data collected by citizen scientists. Those citizen science projects that rely on large-scale data sets, such as Zooniverse, are able to employ statistical and computing tools to assess data quality.

Other evaluation techniques include embedded assessment, which can be built into projects. Becker-Klein et al. (2016) suggest using two different forms of this method: *Performance assessment*, in which participants "do something to demonstrate their knowledge and skills" and *authentic assessment*, "where the learning tasks mirror real-life problem solving situations" (p. 2). They compare this combination of assessment to getting a driver's license in the United States: One takes both a written test on one's knowledge but also an applied driving portion that demonstrates command of driving skills.

As is obvious from this review, some evaluations are highly instrumental and they may not be well matched with projects that value more grassroots, citizen-initiated actions. This is not to say these types of initiatives do not get assessed, but rather that much of citizen science overwhelmingly uses the sort of empirical measures one might expect from this discipline. That said, all citizen science projects are not the same and may have "different motivations, different standards of evidence and different thresholds for action," leading to a need for greater flexibility in assessment (Stilgoe, 2016, para. 11).

Arts

Facing declining audiences along with the rise of participatory practices among ordinary people, traditional visual and fine arts and their supporting institutions are also embracing engagement with audiences in new ways, including a greater emphasis on new forms of collaborative knowledge production (Birchall, 2017). Without widely agreed-upon practices and norms, what constitutes participatory art remains open for debate.

Like citizen journalism, citizen involvement in the creation of visual arts (outside of educational institutions) goes by various names ("community-based art, experiential communities, dialogic art"; Bishop 2012, p. 1) and appears to have struggled even more than journalism to reach a commonly accepted definition. What can be said is that the term "citizen art" is not widely used, and leading scholars such as Bishop (2012) argue for the term "participatory art" in which people are the "medium and the material" (p. 2). According to Finkelpearl (2014) participatory art involves the participation of the artist(s) and ordinary people "referred to as citizens, regular folks, community members, or non-artists [who] interact with professional artists" (p. 2). Participatory art exists in a "liminal space between aesthetics and politics, where the possibility for new forms of interaction and engagement can begin [to] develop" (Miller, 2016, p. 167). It has historically generated less attention within spaces for art that are more commercial (Bishop, 2012), and, in that way, resembles journalism in the constant competition between high-minded goals and commercial imperatives. In fact, participatory art can and has changed the art field by calling into question what can be considered art; as Lave and Wenger (1991/2003) note, practices and actors that challenge the boundaries of a field can generate new ways of thinking about it (see Chapter 5).

For the visual, literary and related arts, Bishop (2012) and others suggest that participatory art has numerous antecedents, such as the Italian Futurists, who reimagined audiences by engaging in behaviors that would inflame or otherwise disturb them with the ultimate aim of "affirming Italy's entry into the modern world through war, technology and destruction" (Bishop, 2012, p. 47). The goal was to provoke audience responses to the ridiculous, often insulting performances or other art forms so that those responses would become part of the art (e.g., throwing vegetables at the artists, joining a riot instigated by the artists). The second World War was followed by increasing levels of commercial culture, eventually prompting an artistic backlash with new forms of participatory art, such as the work of the Situationists in the 1960s (Bishop, 2012). Added to this are the performing arts, which have their own specific history of incorporating audiences into their productions. Genres of performing arts such as applied, popular or development theater and the theater of the oppressed not only include ordinary people in their enactments but also, in some cases, enable participants to draw on their own life experiences in ways that raise their consciousness of their oppression and how it might be challenged. Indeed, these forms of performance art often can be enacted only with the participation of the audience.

Purpose/aims

Citizen participation in the visual arts has been associated with several key aims by the art museums, galleries and related institutions that make public such content. One of these is to embrace participation as a response to changes in population demographics and expectations by new audience members that they are courting (Stallings & Mauldin, 2016). At least in the Western world, with an aging white population, these institutions encourage art projects that aim to appeal to a more diverse, more interactive and younger generation where participation "create[s] art with (not about or for) people not included in traditional museum audiences . . . [to] build social bridges through art" (Finkelpearl, 2014, p. 4). As Miller (2016) explains the aims,

> When Rirkrit Tiravanija sets up a pop-up kitchen at the Venice Biennale, or when Félix González-Torres invites viewers to take from a pile of candy in the corner of a gallery, we are being asked to consider the work of art, not as the dish served up or the piece of candy, but as the various modes of participation, interaction, exchange and relations that such work entails.
>
> (p. 167)

Related to this is another key aim to use art to create social change and, ideally, to make inequities visible in such a way as to ultimately lead to challenging and changing society. More so than much of citizen science, participatory art prioritizes changing participants' ways of being in the world. Often enacted with marginalized groups, much participatory art is viewed as a means to overturn existing hierarchies (Hewitt & Jordan, 2017). The purest forms of this interpretation mean there is no participation for participation's sake but instead the outcome must involve some sort of change (Hewitt & Jordan, 2017). With these more collaborative practices, artists move away from aims to create a static object to be displayed and admired from a distance, and instead they focus their energies on creating relationships with communities. Such art work creates spaces in which social interactions take place that can contribute to building and supporting community networks and fostering new leaders.

Forms of participation

Participatory forms of art are quite diverse and face some of the same questions as citizen journalism. Some forms of participatory art are almost unrecognizable when compared with traditional classic iterations. Finkelpearl (2014) says when the audience becomes "co-producer or participant" in the project, such art consists of a "social space, the interactive moment" (pp. 2, 4). For example, artist Alfredo Jaar gave disposable cameras to residents of a Caracas neighborhood and the images they collected made up the art exhibit he created (Bishop, 2012). In the case of Bateay Srei, a social service non-profit that serves Southeast Asians in Berkeley, California, the organization created an art project that brought together youth and elders in cooking classes combined with youth carrying out oral histories of elders. That said, Literat (2016) argues that much of the participation in art today is a form of crowd sourcing that fosters online citizen contributions to art projects.

Observers such as Finkelpearl (2014) suggest that we think about participatory art as existing in multiple forms and including a range of disparate practices. He argues that participatory art includes "interactive, relational, cooperative, activist, dialogical, and community-based art" (p. 1). These can be combined into three main categories: (1) relational aesthetics, which focuses on relationships with communities/the public as the art; (2) activist participatory act, which works with communities to create change, such as launching a water project in India or an experimental school in Cuba; and (3) antagonistic art, in which the participation may be "destabilizing, contradictory, or antagonistic," such as an exhibit at the Tate Modern in which "mounted police" acting as security on horses randomly herded the audience in meaningless movements (Finkelpearl, 2014, p. 4).

Process, then, is more important than outcome. A well-known project that illustrates this focus was the Project Row House initiative by artist Rick

Loew, who renovated eight shotgun houses in Houston to house artists' work and which grew into a residential/educational space for single mothers, programs for local youth, community housing for low- and middle-income residents, a ballroom for public events and more. The participation of all these people is considered to be part of an ongoing social sculpture in which every person is an artist (Finkelpearl, 2014).

Another project, titled the "Land," was "a collaborative artistic, architectural, and environmental recovery project in Sanpatong, Thailand, [where] residents and artists are welcomed to use a plot of land as a laboratory for development, cultivating rice, building sustainable houses, or channeling solar power" ("Rirkrit Tiravanija," n.d., para. 2). Here again, the challenge to the status quo is the art.

In some of these new forms of participatory art, artists work with community organizations to provide social services and encourage activism from within communities (Birchall, 2017). As noted in the *Encyclopedia of Aesthetics*, "Art can now be a meal, a free school, an immigrant services community center, a dance party or a collectively designed park" (Finkelpearl, 2014, p. 6). As with other disciplines, the levels and amount of participation are debated as is the key question of who initiates the project. As Birchall (2017) argues, many of these projects are "still dependent on the museum as the site of process" (p. 57), which means they are somewhat akin to established news organizations offering websites and apps for citizen journalism to contribute.

Evaluation

With participatory art, evaluation is also debated. Historically, the art field was disciplined by a select circle of critics who decided what was of value following generally agreed-upon understandings of a particular genre's aesthetics. How, then, are these participatory projects that bear little resemblance to traditional work to be judged? Those who were well versed in older understandings of aesthetics are struggling to respond and, indeed, as Bourdieu's (1993) theories would predict, can be resistant to changes, which diminish their expertise, challenge boundaries and bring the very definition of art into question. Likewise, Literat (2012) argues that new forms of participation raise "questions about notions of collective creativity, authorship, collaboration and the shifting structure of artistic production" (p. 2962). As with journalism, many professionals appear to want to maintain ultimate control, and what participatory art reveals are the ways controls are reinforced and tied to existing institutions.

As participatory art defuses individual authorship, not only does the product change but also how it can and should be evaluated must adapt.

For many traditional critics, the shift of fine and visual art to activity thus raises the question of what makes this art and something of value (Miller, 2016). Pointing out that all participatory art is neither equal nor successful, Bishop (2012) too asks how might it be critiqued. Of particular concern is if the project is created offsite and only the results are displayed in galleries for audiences, thus leaving the key parts of the creation unseen and impossible to evaluate. Oftentimes, an artist initiates the project and thus is considered the creator, despite arguments that the work can exist only with community participation.

Others argue that participation has become so *de rigueur* that it is oftentimes no longer subversive but instead reinforces the status quo. Indeed, critics from the UK in particular argue participation has been co-opted through Third Way cultural policies that ultimately seek to control art and artists (Birchall, 2017; Hewitt & Jordan, 2017). They suggest participation has become part of the neo-liberal mantra of generating a creative economy where art becomes "boosterism, [that can] appropriate community voices" (Finkelpearl, 2014, p. 5). In this case, Hewitt and Jordan (2017) argue projects are judged only on the level of participation even though in their opinion, "participation is not a value in itself but depends entirely on the value of the project in which the participation takes place" (p. 3). In sum, the evaluation of participatory art remains highly contested.

Ultimately, participatory art is torn between seemingly competing aims: a strategy to adapt to the changing market or a means to create social change (Stallings & Mauldin, 2016). In other words, is the goal to make more money or is it to build a better society? Institution-initiated citizen journalism faces the same issues. Do professional news outlets ultimately pay attention to citizen journalism to protect the field and thus their commercial dominance over public information or are they interacting with it to contribute to more lofty goals?

Lessons for citizen journalism

How might these two very different disciplines help mainstream news media view citizen journalism and participation in the news differently? Here, I lay out some lessons learned.

1   Citizen science makes it a point to foster support for the discipline by sharing how to use its methods and making structured opportunities available to do so. It further seeks to create positive attitudes toward the natural world, and to promote environmental stewardship practices and attitudes. When offered by traditional news outlets, citizen journalism opportunities also often attempt to train or at least offer guidance

in how to carry out journalism, but the news industry in general does not appear to see this as recruiting the public to become stewards of the news. Perhaps more emphasis needs to be placed on civic responsibility and less on the individual's enactment. Also, by handing over much of the socialization and "training" to platforms, news organizations may be losing an opportunity to promote a clearer understanding of what journalism does and a sense of civic responsibility involved in creating public information. Indeed, news literacy has been left to academic and non-profit organizations that emphasize critical readings, which some of its proponents now reject as merely making the public distrust the news media (boyd, 2017).

2   Citizen science has a strong emphasis on formal assessment techniques. This is aided by strong institutional support by non-commercial entities, such as governments and non-profit community organizations. Professional journalism in most countries has neither the resources nor in some cases the skills to carry out consistent and ongoing assessment of their citizen and participatory projects. However, they could do so by partnering with academics from journalism or media studies or even education and other fields.

3   Citizen science has developed ethical guidelines, such as the European Citizen Science Association's Principles of Citizen Science. Citizen journalism has no common set of ethical principles.

4   Citizen science accepts that citizen contributions may not be entirely accurate and they address this in some cases by using enormous data sets where such anomalies can be identified via statistical formulas. This may not be as realistic for news organizations, whose own verification practices range from in-house practices to subscribing to outside verification entities, such as Storyful; however, as Big Data plays an ever growing role in journalism, this may become a reality for mainstream news as well.

5   Participatory art is about relationships and the process of creating the art. In citizen journalism, there needs to be greater emphasis on relationships as a key product or outcome. Robinson and DeShano (2011) and Borger Van Hoof and Sanders (2016a) found ordinary people interacting with journalists in participatory news contexts have expectations of a more interactive, equitable relationship, while Lewis, Holton and Coddington (2016) argue that reciprocity "is a key ingredient for the development of trust, connectedness and social capital" (p. 2).

6   Some academic disciplines associated with the arts have responded to the rise of participation by creating new programs, such as Social Practice, that train artists in the skills needed to reimagine art as a relationship to interact with communities. In journalism, a handful of

universities have taught citizen journalism or related courses in the early days of its development, but overall universities have followed the lead of the profession, seeing citizen content producers as interlopers to be tamed through verification and other means. This does not help them to respond to this phenomenon in a way that could benefit both citizens and the profession, perhaps by attracting new audiences and supporting positive civic engagement.

5 Schooling citizen journalists

One of the ways that ordinary people become citizen journalists is through participating in one of the various journalism training programs found around the world. Some of these provide face-to-face education supported by non-profit institutions, ranging from NGOs to universities to public service media. Other in-person trainings are offered by hyperlocal news outlets and other commercial entities. In addition, many traditional news outlets offer online tutorials and other similarly self-directed forums for ordinary people to teach themselves; in part this is because of the potentially large number of participants but also it suggests that such training is not seen as a priority. A less frequent approach has been the offering of citizen journalism training via massive online open courses (MOOCs), such as "Journalism Skills for Engaged Citizens," taught by professors from the University of Melbourne on the Coursera platform. Still other forms of learning how to be a citizen journalist are self-activated in which citizens school themselves in part by observing what others in their networks do in a form of "practice proxies" (Kus et al., 2017; Mugar, Østerlund, Hassman, Crowston, & Jackson, 2014, p. 111).

Much citizen journalism training is not guided by any explicit theories of learning. Thus, in this chapter I lay out a framework for thinking about the ways citizens may gain knowledge of journalism practices drawing on the learning theories developed by Lave and Wenger (1991/2003) on formal and informal learning practices. Concentrating on training may suggest ways citizen and professional journalists can come together to develop more inclusive journalism practices and perhaps generate greater trust. In connection with the rest of this volume, training and other initiatives for citizen journalists can also be seen as forms of boundary work. Learning theories can provide us with a perspective on the ways boundaries and their peripheries are challenged and reinforced via formal and informal schooling of citizen journalists. Wenger (1998a, 1998b) writes that boundaries are actually sites of learning that offer opportunities for communities to remain adaptable, arguing that "This permeable periphery creates many opportunities for learning, as outsiders and newcomers learn the practice in concrete terms, and core members gain new insights from contacts with less-engaged participants" (p. 4).

Situated learning, communities of practice

The concept of situated learning posits that people learn through being engaged in an activity rather than passively receiving knowledge (Lave & Wenger, 1991/2003). This view of learning stresses participation and relationships as learners gain knowledge not from a top-down transmission of information but rather from being part of communities of others engaged in the pursuit of a common goal. As Wenger (1998a, 1998b) argues, learning is often viewed as an individual act, but, in reality, as social beings, people learn collaboratively and, in doing so, may sustain or produce a community. This is how knowledge is passed on; the "larger community of practitioners reproduces itself" through sharing knowledge with newcomers (Hanks, 1991/2003, p. 16).

More specifically, Lave and Wenger (1991/2003) argue that situated learning takes place within communities of practice (CoP), which are "a set of relations among persons, activity, and world" (Lave & Wenger, 1991/2003, p. 98). More precisely, a CoP consists of a joint enterprise, which is a shared endeavor continually negotiated by its members bound together by relationships of mutual engagement while employing a shared repertoire of communal resources (routines, artifacts, sensibilities, etc.) over time (Wenger, 1998a). "Participants in communities of practice learn how to fit in, how to contribute and how to change their community" (Aubrey & Riley, 2015, p. 173). Within journalism studies, the CoP concept has been used to aid our understanding of the practices of journalists, including ethnic media professionals (e.g., Husband, 2005; Matsaganis & Katz, 2014), as well as the ways a CoP approach can help us understand how professional journalists adapt to new practices as journalism becomes increasingly digitized (e.g., Schmitz Weiss & Domingo, 2010). One gap in this area of study is the ways amateurs and ordinary people learn to perform as citizen journalists even though in many cases they are not entirely part of professional journalism communities nor even welcome to be part of them.

Learners

Of particular interest here is Lave and Wenger's (1991/2003) study of apprentices across a variety of domains and the commonalities in the ways that newcomers learned their crafts. Interestingly, there is also a history of viewing journalism as a craft and not a profession (see Splichal & Dahlgren, 2016). These scholars introduced the concept of legitimate peripheral participation (LPP) to describe the position of these learners, who are located at the boundaries of various CoPs. While the label "legitimate" can be a judgmental means of marking boundaries, it is used by Lave and Wenger to indicate the learner is being schooled in a specific body of practices by those with more experience and knowledge, with the expected result that what they learn will be deemed acceptable by those already expert in the practices of that community. With training, they will come to be seen as legitimate. Thus, LPP is "not a structure . . . but a way of acting in the world" that helps to explain how newcomers to a CoP engage at the boundaries of that community (Lave & Wenger, 1991/2003, p. 25). Although they are often viewed only as at the borders of the CoP, these newcomers may still contribute to the community (Lave & Wenger, 1991/2003). This clearly also applies to citizen journalists on the periphery of the professional journalism community as they too can produce content and even potentially impact the "legitimate" practitioners' work.

More specifically Wenger (1998a, p. 5) argues that learning is carried out across the following dimensions:

- Identity. A learner creates an identity by developing a personal history of becoming within a community.
- Community. When participating in a shared joint enterprise, one's participation may come to be viewed as competent and thus enables acceptance within the community.
- Practice. Practices are learned by talking about the community's "shared historical and social resources, frameworks and perspectives" that can enable them to engage in actions common to the community.
- Meaning. To learn is to be able to experience the world individually and collectively while engaging with it in meaningful ways.

In addition, learning by apprentices and other types of newcomers to a CoP takes place within a "learning architecture" consisting of three dimensions (Wenger, 1998a, p. 271): (a) places of engagement; (b) materials and experiences with which to build an image of the world; and (c) ways of having an effect on the work and making one's actions matter.

Just as professional journalism seeks to maintain legitimacy by policing its borders, legitimate peripheral participation (LPP) is also about legitimization as a key practice in maintaining authority and power by members of a community. It is important to note that as newcomers interact with a CoP, that community and its activities are not static but instead constantly changing in part due to these interactions. For example, this may occur when newcomers ask questions about practices that have been internalized by members for so long that they become invisible. We see this in journalism practices such as the tendency to trust the word of official sources before that of an ordinary person.

A CoP, then, is characterized by its negotiability, or the ways in which newcomers at its borders can contribute to changes within the community. We have seen that the arrival of newcomers or interlopers at the border of the journalistic community has contributed to new practices and new ways of thinking about professional identities. Thus, the enactment of LPP can be both empowering and disempowering; it contributes to enabling entry into a community but also may contribute to shaping what practices qualify for acceptance or even if practices will be accepted or interlopers admitted.

Belonging to a community is about achieving competence in its ways of doing things. At the boundaries, Wenger (1998b) suggests, competence and experience may separate. In fact, if competence and experience are too closely aligned, learning might not take place and the community will become static. Likewise, if competence and experience are too far apart, learning also cannot take place either, as there is no common understanding point. While acknowledging that boundaries divide, Wenger (1998b) argues that they can also inspire new ways of thinking within a community that otherwise would not occur.

LPP and online training: proxy practices

Some researchers argue that new variations on LPP need to be considered to be more applicable to the online environment. Mugar et al. (2014) studied how learning takes place within online citizen science projects. They found that just as with face-to-face apprenticeships, participants move toward more sustained engagements in which they become more knowledgeable about "tasks [and] vocabulary" (p. 110). They found online participants on the platform Zooniverse who may never interact directly with an expert learn in two main ways: through their own participation and through being exposed to the participation of others. This "does not happen through instructions of teaching about the practice but only through specific and contextualized discussions and stories told within practice" (p. 110). Within Zooniverse, learning specifically took place via the discussion boards and forums hosting more than 1 million citizen science contributions. The researchers introduce the term "practice proxies" for talking about the ways practices might be passed on without directly sharing them in a face-to-face workshop or similar real-world forum. Instead, "system features . . . make visible the socially salient aspects of people's unfolding work practices rather than aspects of the practices directly" (p. 110). That is, norms are implied in the finished contributions of fellow citizens and mastering these helps newcomers establish credibility and competence. Mugar et al.'s (2014) work helps explain the unseen pedagogy that produces much independently produced citizen journalism, such as Black Twitter. While online learning may take place via sites and apps that help orient ordinary people to expectations of the field through tutorials and other learning devices as noted earlier, learners also pick up on practices through observations within social media (Kus et al., 2017). Here, the platform provides a design that shapes behavior for those producing citizen journalism, but it is also the other participants who provide indirect instruction through example and by engaging with others in discussions that clarify their aims and practices.

How citizen journalists learn

In what follows, I draw on Lave and Wenger's (1991/2003) ideas to consider existing research on citizen journalism training from different contexts to illustrate how they engage citizens in situated learning environments. Examining various reported accounts of citizen journalism training as well as websites that offer training or provide access to artifacts that offer training (e.g., tip sheets) from around the world, I focused on three elements highlighted by Wenger (1998a) as key sites for learning: identity, practice and community. Obviously, not all programs provide opportunities in each area for all participants, but it can be helpful to consider the ways that they do so.

Identity

Learning can change who we are and how we see ourselves and learning can sometimes result in developing a new identity. For example, when ordinary people with disabilities were trained to be citizen journalists in the UK, the participants initially lacked self-confidence and were afraid to exercise a public voice (Luce, Jackson, & Thorsen, 2017). The fears experienced by this marginalized population were hardened and difficult to overcome. Yet, as the disabled participants engaged in mastering practices of journalism, they changed their views of themselves, becoming more confident as they came to see themselves as able to engage in and be identified as citizen journalists. As Luce and colleagues (2017) argue, forming a new identity in this way can be a "transformative" experience (p. 279). New identities appear to be shaped by forging new connections with others engaged in similar work and through being exposed to models for new behaviors.

Fostering connections

Face-to-face citizen journalism training generally revolves around some sort of workshop(s), seminars or related type of session. Common sites for training include universities, libraries and other community spaces. The UK project that carried out citizen journalism training for people with disabilities took place across five workshops over two months at a university, while other trainings for homeless citizen journalists were held in a public library. Taiwan's Public Service Television citizen journalism program PeoPo has held more than 500 training sessions across the country, sponsored summer camps for citizen journalists and also established 14 citizen journalism press centers at university journalism departments, along with training in how to teach citizen journalism at community colleges (Hung, 2015). In the UK, the hyperlocal newspaper *Jesmond Local* collaborated with university students to run boot camps (Baines & Li, 2013), while the Winnipeg Community News Commons held workshops on photography, video and audio as well as storytelling in the city library and at a local community newspaper's café. India's CGNet Swara citizen journalism program has held more than "50 multi-day workshops that have trained over 2,000 community members and social activists about the goals of CGNet and how to record reports on the system" (Marathe, O'Neill, Pain, & Thies, 2015, p. 3). Its recruitment of participants and provision of initial training are a highly visible act of public inclusion. "CGNET trainers walk into hamlets and villages, beat on drums, use puppets to encourage people to use the service. Anyone can ask questions and people are given simple tips on how to report and post stories" (Pain, 2017, p. 11).

Many journalism training programs seek to create connections among participants through these various workshops, conferences, meetings and social events. Initiatives such as Taiwan's PeoPo and Colombia's state-sponsored effort to establish citizen radio stations throughout the country both held national conferences to bring together citizen participants. These and other types of meetings at various levels, including the regional and local community levels, provide opportunities for citizen journalists to share ideas and dialogue as well as to create networks among participants (Baroni & Mayr, 2017; Hung-lo, 2012; Davis, 2017).

Even meetings at the local level can lead to new connections and relationships. A participant in the Winnipeg Community News Commons citizen journalism project described one of their meetings:

> There were no attitudes here and our monthly story meetings were so much fun. Everyone sitting around the board table in The Winnipeg

Foundation's office on the 13th floor of the Richardson Building had a chance to speak. We went around the table and each person talked about stories they were working on or were going to be working on . . . I had no idea that such a strong community of writers and (citizen journalists) existed and I'm so glad I found it.

(Hawe, 2017, para. 23, 25)

Modeling

The second means for creating identity was to model journalistic practices and values. One of the key ways this was done was via coaching and mentoring sessions that not only helped those learning citizen journalism boost their practical skills but also inspired them to develop the confidence necessary to carry out their work. In Winnipeg, a citizen journalist described coaching as supportive and contributing to a collaborative atmosphere: "Our editor would take our ideas and expand on them for us and others would interject with positive suggestions" (Hawe, 2017, para. 24). In some cases, editors or other experts edited or otherwise helped shape citizen work to meet professional ideals and standards. Programs often provide not just a workshop but also one-one-one editing and coaching. For example, the non-profit organization Paper Airplanes, which partnered with Northeastern University to offer citizen journalism training in the Middle East, included one-on-one peer mentors. Professionals might help develop story ideas, fact check articles and encourage amateurs to get out into the community and report. A professional editor overseeing the Reporter Corps citizen program in the United States set up workshops with city officials as a means of introducing these local decision makers to the citizen reporters (Gerson, Chen, Wenzel, Ball-Rokeach, & Parks, 2017). This sort of mentoring may also serve as a form of reciprocity between professional journalists and non-professionals. This is important because such engagement can have long-term benefits in terms of professionals coming to better understand their communities and of participants developing trust in the established journalists (Borger et al., 2016a; Lewis et al., 2016).

Not all training is in person. In fact, much training is offered via online tutorials. The forms may include a hyperlocal news operation providing a tip sheet or a larger international news site such as the *GuardianWitness* offering its own "Tips and Tricks" webpage. In the summer of 2018, *GuardianWitness* featured three videos for citizen contributors to view: one on lighting, one on sound and one on verification of content. The sound tutorial page told participants,

Your sound is just as important as your picture when shooting video. Here, *Guardian* multimedia producer Elliot Smith introduces some of the different types of sound you might encounter and get some top tips from sound industry veteran Nigel Woodford of Richmond Film Services. This video is part of a series of video production primers to help you contribute to *GuardianWitness*. Find out how to send us your video.

(Sound Recording: A *GuardianWitness* Guide to Making Great Video, n.d., para. 1–2)

In a multination study of European citizen journalists, Kus and colleagues (2017) found that volunteer content contributors often had no official training and, instead, many relied on what they characterize as "improvisation" techniques. Here, citizen journalists receive "implicit training" when their content is posted online (Kus et al., 2017, p. 11). This can happen by observing and mimicking what others do but also through noting likes, retweets and other forms of social media approval, which can lead individuals to shape their behavior to match these forms of endorsement, forms that originate not with existing journalism organizations but with social media platforms. Citizen journalists are also found to gravitate toward self-training by visiting specialized journalism sites or blogs that they told researchers they go to in order to learn more about how to participate in the journalism community. In other words, amateur journalists like citizen scientists learned via Mugar et al.'s (2012) proxy practices too.

Practices

Participants in training become aware of the field's competences through a conceptual understanding of shared "historical, social resources, frameworks and perspectives" that in many cases are embedded in the practical skills that journalists are expected to become proficient in (Wenger, 1998a, p. 5). One of the main ways this occurs is through a focus on teaching technical skills, such how to frame a still image, how to ask a source questions and other basic reporting practices. Becoming proficient in these skills is a way for apprentices and other newcomers to establish the competence expected in order to become part of the journalism CoP. Citizen journalism training programs tend to offer schooling in these skills via two different frameworks: professionalization and conscientization.

Professionalization

The aim of many citizen journalism training initiatives is to bring the citizen practitioners into the same set of values and practices of mainstream journalism. For example, a Michigan citizen journalism news site, *The Rapidian*, features a page titled, "Citizen Journalism 101: Tips for Producing a Good Story," where newcomers are offered advice such as how to fact check a story and schooled in norms such as why news stories need more than one source ("Stories with only one source, no matter how important, always appear weak and one-sided").

Many citizen journalism programs aim to inculcate the amateur news producers they train with mainstream professional values, and such training often focuses on technical skills as well as traditional journalism usage of them.

The BBC's Arabic section developed a citizen journalism program in which participants would be "'citizen producers' and inducted into the BBC's professional journalistic ethos" (Gillespie, 2013, p. 106). As part of the training, they had to carry out background research providing "reliable evidence in the form of quotes from newspaper articles, TV clips or weblinks to articles or reports" (p. 106). Likewise, the Institute for War and Peace Reporting's citizen journalism trainers reported that they taught objectivity in order to move participants away from voicing claims and accusations to instead practice a more professional form of journalism (Yousuf & Taylor, 2017). The training was based on the belief that this focus was important for citizen journalists in conflict areas such as Syria so that citizen reporters could learn to bring groups together and provide cohesion within a community by negotiating multiple points of view (Yousuf & Taylor, 2017). In these sorts of programs where citizen journalists may be initiated into professional news values, this may change their self-identities, re-orienting participants from seeing themselves mainly as activists speaking for one side to more cautious and perhaps distanced observers.

Even with younger participants, training might prioritize basic values, sometimes quite harshly. In the case of a Brazilian citizen journalism project aimed at students, school administrators burned a student-produced newspaper in a public space because it contained grammatical errors that they claimed "would create a poor image of the school" (Bailey, 2009, p. 139). In contrast, a newspaper run by Rhodes University in South Africa sought to interest area youth in citizen journalism by hosting training workshops taught by university students on topics such as how to produce content in a range of genres, which were specially adapted to appeal to youth, such as reporting mini stories and reporting via haiku. At the same time, the program emphasized the rights and responsibilities of citizenship (Berger, 2012). This suggests a sort of bridging of professionalism with consciousness raising.

Conscientization

Citizen journalism programs in South America often draw from Friere's *conscientization* theories to awaken the critical consciousness of local residents. Such training aims for more than instilling professional practices in participants but instead prioritizes empowerment (Rodriguez, 2011). Participants in the *Viva Comunidade* public health program trained health workers to be citizen journalists with a conceptual guide, "Citizenship, Human Rights and Participatory Culture," which focused in part on providing background on the history of the local community and the ways citizen journalism could serve it (Davis, 2017). The training guide suggests a central role for the citizen journalist as someone who could explain the community to itself and others. The course content blended a review of the ways citizen media had long been produced within the favelas, along with Western sources, such as Dan Gillmor's *We the Media* book. Participants wrote reflection papers on human rights as well as honing their awareness of favela stereotypes.

A community photography program also in Brazil's favelas sought to help the residents learn to produce what is called "shared photography," in which those being photographed are not the object of the photo but collaborate in producing its meaning. The focus is not on objectivity or professional values but on reaching people who are ignored or maligned in most of Brazil's mainstream news coverage (Baroni & Mayr, 2017). The program's philosophy is that when stories of marginalized people are told with respect, that can transform both outsider understandings of the community and its understanding of itself. Training for citizen reporters in India's CGNet Swara program also sought a form of *conscientization* by constantly emphasizing that reporting was an act of citizenship that the participants were entitled to be able to do; thus, teachers told those receiving training, "'*Haq se mangiye!*' (These are your rights. Ask for them boldly!)" (Pain, 2017, p. 10). When asked about their participation, citizen journalists often shared the thinking of this participant who said, "Creating news for CGNET is sometimes a way for us to understand our problem better. For example, now it's no longer about not getting water. It's about first articulating and then demanding our right to clean water" (Pain, 2017, p. 11).

Community

One of the most effective forms of recognition is for citizen stories to be shared with audiences, often through publication/airing/posting or other forms of amplification by professional news media or other information sites. The Institute for War and Peace Reporting's Syria Project posts citizen content onto its project-specific website, Damascus Bureau, as well as

IWPR's main website. Further, it connects the citizen journalists with international news media, which also sometimes publish their work. Participants in the non-profit Paper Airplanes citizen journalism program have had articles about health care and ongoing violence in Ghouta, Syria, published by Global Voices and the *New York Times*. They also partnered with Global Student Square to establish an ongoing pipeline for their graduates' content.

Programs may sometimes pay participants for their work. Even if the amounts are nominal, this may contribute to the process of bringing amateurs into the realm of professional journalism. In some cases, the citizen journalists are paid simply for participating if not directly for their work. For example, the U.S. program Reporter Corps aimed at youth requires that they apply and go through a selection process that, if successful, means they get a stipend. Nairobi's citizen journalism project *Sauti ya Mtaa* ("Voices of the Streets") also paid citizen contributors a small fee, which was a crucial form of support for some (Maracci, 2016). For the most disadvantaged, these payments enable them to participate, a fact that training programs sometimes overlook. Such recognition can be important forms of "stratified legitimacy," which indicates a semi-mastery of competencies, reflected, for example, in allowing participants who have demonstrated mastery of at least some skills to edit other's work (Goodwin, Pope, Mort, & Smith, 2005, p. 863). Still other forms of recognition include Taiwan PeoPo's awards or the T-shirts and certificates presented at the end of the South African youth program training (Berger, 2012).

At its heart, the provision of citizen journalism training is often motivated by what is considered a common aim of many professional journalists: to give a voice to those who are often unheard and under-represented. In the best cases of professional-amateur interactions, professionals seek to share practices with the amateur reporters that are intended to equip ordinary people to reach that goal. After all, the trainers are not looking to apprentice investigative reporters but rather community voices. Thus, the competency that they often hope to foster is that of raising such voices to public attention in the form of new narratives and perspectives from the grassroots – whether these are third-person accounts or the citizens' relaying of their own personal stories. In this way, training may contribute to bolstering self-esteem and the confidence to engage with civic issues (Luce et al., 2017). This self-confidence to have a say in a community's problems using newly learned practices, then, may be the ultimate competence.

Conclusions: change at the boundaries

At certain points during some of the training initiatives outlined here, we see moments of conflict – the ferment at the periphery as newcomers push

against existing practices. Responses to these conflicts are important to consider because in a healthy CoP, the experts in established practices must be
willing to adapt and change in order to continue to be co-learners in their
own field. In one of Brazil's citizen journalism favela programs, the trainer
wanted the newcomers to narrow their stories so that topics matched the
program sponsor's agenda; yet that was not the student participants' preferred sort of story. In response to their resistance, the trainer retreated to a
harder embrace of the traditional practices (Davis, 2017).

In other cases, the skills being taught were changed because of the prefer-
ences of the citizen journalism learners. For example, in the South African
citizen reporter program to train youth to report local news, the trainers
found that student participants did not use full sentences or complete words,
instead relying on an abbreviated slang. Rather than hewing to traditional
professionalism as was done in the Brazilian health reporting program, the
creators here noted that professionals and others needed to adapt to the
citizen's ways of communication in order to bring under-heard voices into
public conversations. Indeed, the trainers took the unusual step of teaching haiku as a possible journalistic genre for those reasons. In this way,
they have answered Kus and colleagues' (2017) call to create a dialogue
"between journalism's center and periphery" (p. 14). According to Lave
and Wenger (1991/2003) identity is about seeing oneself as a member of
the community, and we often assume that all citizen reporters, if given a
chance, would like to join the professional journalism community when
what they really may desire is simply to belong to any community.

6   Conclusion

Citizen journalism has never been a unitary phenomenon; instead, it inhabits a seemingly endless array of forms. This volume has steered part of its focus toward two specific iterations of citizen journalism that seek to document and sometimes participate in or even precipitate change, be it a quest for social justice by the engaged citizen journalist or the pursuit of a takedown of the current professional news system by the enraged citizen journalist. These forms are not the products of solicitations by mainstream news media but have been conjured into existence by interlopers, renegades, inbetweeners and other outsiders at the borders of the profession. With most fields, and journalism is no exception, we tend to focus on the center, where power resides and norms are established and protected, but it is increasingly clear that the edges are where we can identify both threats and also possibilities. In these spaces, we will discover new forms of journalism worth supporting and those of which we need to be wary.

The engaged citizen journalist is sympathetic to or even participates in social justice movements and other forms of activism that aim to raise the voices of marginalized groups and/or protect them from acts of aggression and oppression. In doing so, their work may contribute to their own self-efficacy as these citizen journalists are sometimes themselves disenfranchised members of society. Positioned at the margins of professional journalism, they chart new narratives and challenge old ones and, in this way, can also play a role in collective endeavors that can contribute to community building. Engaged citizen journalists are often marked by a commitment to creating change through social justice. Their identities are not rigid, as seen in this self-effacing quote from live streamer Jon Zielger, describing himself as a "journalist, citizen journalist, a live streamer . . . a dude with a phone" (Lisenby, 2017, para. 2). Which of those he is depends on the moment he finds himself in. Many engaged citizen journalists are ambivalent about the title, opting for labels connected with the form they prefer to use in their reporting, such as live streamer and blogger. Engaged citizen journalists often work independently of any organization without financial or other types of support. As Ferguson live streamer Bassem Masri explained, "We ain't have no backup, no money" (Voices on Ferguson and Police Accountability, 2015). In this way, they become more dependent on the communities within which they are embedded, crowd-funding financial contributions and building personal connections with audiences.

The enraged citizen journalists often express aggrieved points of view, which they may articulate through a nationalistic voice. They see themselves as truth tellers threatened by the same under-served communities the engaged journalists often represent (non-white, immigrant, etc.). Enraged citizen journalists see themselves as objects of oppression, under attack from government, social movements (particularly those supporting ethnic and/or gender causes) and particularly from a lack of acceptance by the mainstream news media. These citizen journalists operate like termites, eating the institutions and practices that support existing norms hollow. Eldridge (2018) warns we must take care not to dismiss these kinds of interlopers at the edges of the profession even when their interpretations of journalism strain the bounds of "decency" (p. 3). Others argue that giving them consideration only increases the acceptance of their extremism (Phillips, 2018). Whichever the case, their identities are boldly performed, sometimes with theatrics that leave those they have focused their fire on singed out of their reputations, their jobs or perhaps even the public sphere entirely. Unlike the engaged citizen journalists, they are able to access resources such that some among them have received funding for their reporting from conservative billionaires, including the forty-fifth president of the United States. The scrappy citizen underdog label they so gladly embrace can at times seem perversely Orwellian.

Both forms – the engaged and the enraged – have come about in part due to the failures of mainstream journalism to think more broadly about how to respond to the changing nature of news into forms that do not necessarily conform to our historic understandings. As Gowing (2014) argues, the information space itself is changing, but established institutions including but not limited to the news media seem incapable of recognizing the extent of the challenge to their authority. Granted, in the United States, much of the news industry has been decimated economically by the ongoing takeover of their advertising revenue and their audiences by new media behemoths that are more powerful and pervasive than any of the old news providers ever were. Added to this was the 2008 economic crisis that served to intensify these patterns. This left little energy to confront what seemed like more existential issues taking place at the profession's borders.

Now, we see the threat to mainstream news media has deepened considerably with a growing sense that the performance of journalism by many enraged citizen journalists, sometimes promoting absurd and sometimes dangerous twists of reality, has become accepted ways of talking about serious public matters for some audiences. For many people, these actors are their dominant information sources, existing in an increasingly closed information ecology (Faris et al., 2017). The acceptance of falsehoods has expanded beyond these newcomers to professional outlets. Witness the requirement that newscasters working for the conservative Sinclair Broadcasting Group, which owns 193 local television news stations in the United States and thus is a main information source in many communities, give on-air statements that factual stories that don't comport with the owner's political beliefs are not true (Chang, 2018). Thus, the industry disruptions are here for all to see, but as Nagle (2017) notes, the optimists thought the "old hierarchical models would be replaced by the wisdom of the crowd, the swarm, the hive mind, citizen journalism and user generated content. They got their wish but it's not quite the utopian version they were hoping for" (p. 3). What exactly comes next remains an open question.

Missed opportunities

In considering how other fields have responded to the rise of citizen participation we see that the fine and visual arts have found creative ways to reinvent themselves such that their very productions can be animated only by public involvement. At the same time, some artists and institutions have turned the profession away from commercial control to focus on participation as a means to achieve social change. In the arena of science, ordinary people are invited to observe and document the natural world, which today is experiencing its own life and death crisis in the form of climate change. Through citizen science participation, some people see themselves as stewards of the environment and even the discipline of science itself. These are paths that the field of journalism does not appear to have taken: declaring an important iteration of their product must be animated by the public's participation. Likewise, journalism has not consistently sought to nurture a corps of amateur enthusiasts who believe in journalism itself (not a particular news outlet or story) and who could advocate for the importance of news or even facts with the public.

In the educational realm, the arts have responded to the rise of participation with a new area of study at universities through which they train artists to work with communities: the Social Practice in the Arts degree. Yet most journalism educational institutional programs have not opted to follow this sort of path. Participation in the news has not become a key emphasis in most journalism curriculums, much less a new degree. Instead, the opposite has often occurred: reinforcing a line between formal, professional journalism and those forms at the edges. We see here the promotion of practices that draw deeper lines between everyday content makers and professionals, such as the embrace of virtual reality and other expensive technologies. Meanwhile, citizen science has become so widely accepted in many schools that educators have developed specific assessment tools to measure its success in meeting its goals.

In terms of training citizen journalists, here too lies a missed opportunity. Much of the training offered to citizens is through impersonal online tutorials designed to be useful to a homogenous mass of participants. Such training is not aimed at establishing reciprocal connections that would bring citizens into a more meaningful, stronger relationship with journalism, a connection with the field that could contribute to greater trust. The other common form of "training" comes via the proxies identified by Mugar et al. (2014) and Kus et al. (2017) through which citizens simply observe what others do on social media platforms and imitate them. In this way, the platform's own affordances and norms combined with how certain users create and post content can become widespread behaviors. While interactions online can be reciprocal in positive ways (e.g., Harte, Williams, & Turner, 2017; Freelon et al., 2018), unfortunately, much of what is mimicked may fail to contribute to the public good and may even be damaging to societies (e.g., Marwick & Lewis, 2017).

When successful, face-to-face trainings represent a different option: ordinary people including those from marginalized communities building relationships with each other and their communities, becoming more effective, confident citizens. In the non-Western examples, we especially see a greater willingness to experiment with creative new approaches. While it's true that being part of a community of practice could possibly serve to domesticate citizen practitioners, in the best cases it may create opportunities for journalism to be a joint endeavor with citizens to improve local communities. Training that aims to create social change for the betterment of a community may well be the means to work with engaged citizens. The concept of the CoP also offers different ways to think about the functions of borders and how to make them productive spaces rather than walls of separation.

More creative and personal-oriented training and similar interactions could help to create a corps of news stewards for journalism or at least supporters of the importance of factual public information that aims to solve problems, not contribute to them. Such stewardship could be useful in challenging a U.S. president who publicly calls the news media the "enemy of the people." While this may not stop attacks against journalism, in a time of crisis, stewards of the news may make such actions less acceptable. In sum, the community that needs to be built is not for an individual news organization's website but for journalism itself.

Final thoughts

Whether normalized by mainstream news media, socialized by media educators, or criticized by governments and other elites, citizen journalism will remain a powerful social and political force, albeit one that appears in a range of genres across many different places. From the heart of liberal democracies to the dangerous shoals of authoritarian regimes, its roles are dependent on who is enacting it, for what reasons and with what aim. This book ends with the declaration that we must accept that news as we have known it for more than a century as a particular sort of cultural product may in some not too distant future change into a quite different, perhaps unrecognizable form. If so, we need to understand the potential and the perils of multiple forms of citizen journalism and consider the steps that could be taken to shepherd their production of journalism – or something similar that consists of factual content necessary to enable the sharing of public information – to successful new configurations.

References

Ahva, L. (2017). How Is participation practiced by "in-betweeners" of journalism? *Journalism Practice, 11*(2–3), 142–159.

Al-Ghazzi, O. (2014). Citizen journalism' in the Syrian uprising: Problematizing Western narratives in a local context. *Communication Theory, 24*(4), 435–454.

Allan, S. (2006). *Online news: Journalism and the Internet.* Maidenhead: Open University.

Allan, S. (2015). Introduction: Photojournalism and citizen journalism. *Journalism Practice, 9*(4), 455–464.

Allan, S., & Thorsen, E. (Eds.). (2009). *Citizen journalism global perspectives.* New York: Peter Lang.

Anderson, C. W. (2013). *Rebuilding the news: Metropolitan journalism in the digital age.* Philadelphia: Temple University Press.

Anderson, E. (2015). The white space. *Sociology of Race and Ethnicity, 1*(1), 10–21.

Anzaldua, G. (1987). *Borderlands: The new mestiza = La frontera* (1st ed.). San Francisco: Spinsters, Aunt Lute.

Araiza, J. A., Sturm, H. A., Istek, P., & Bock, M. A. (2016). Hands up, don't shoot, whose side are you on? Journalists tweeting the Ferguson protests. *Cultural Studies? Critical Methodologies, 16*(3), 305–312.

Atlas, R. & Pollard, S. (Directors & Producers). (2017). *Acorn and the Firestorm.* [DVD]. United States: First Run Features.

Aubrey, K., & Riley, A. (2015). *Understanding and using educational theories.* Thousand Oaks: Sage.

Bailey, O. G. (2009). Citizen journalism and child rights in Brazil. In S. Allan & E. Thorsen (Eds.), *Citizen journalism: Global perspectives* (pp. 133–142). New York: Peter Lang.

Baines, D., & Li, T. (2013, June 3–5). *Students teaching in the community: Building employability, social sustainability and "journalism as process".* A paper presented at the World Journalism Education Conference, Mechelen, Belgium. Retrieved from http://wjec.be/downloads

Balek, T. (2015, May 1). "Happy warriors" converge on Washington, DC for right online blogger conference. *WatchDog.org.* Retrieved from www.watchdog.org/opinion/happy-warriors-converge-on-washington-dc-for-rightonline-blogger-conference/article_db4379ba-ed15-5cf1-a9d9-4597be931e4d.html

Barnard, S. R. (2018). Tweeting# Ferguson: Mediatized fields and the new activist journalist. *New Media & Society, 20*(7), 2252–2271.

Baroni, A., & Mayr, A. (2017). "Shared photography" (Photo) journalism and political mobilisation in Rio de Janeiro's favelas. *Journalism Practice, 11*(2–3), 285–301.

Beam, C. (2010, July 22). Breitbart's back: The man behind the Shirley Sherrod shakeup. *Slate*. Retrieved from www.slate.com/articles/news_and_politics/recycled/2010/07/breitbarts_back.html

Becker-Klein, R., Peterman, K., & Stylinski, C. (2016). Embedded assessment as an essential method for understanding public engagement in citizen science. *Citizen Science: Theory and Practice, 1*(1), 8. http://doi.org/10.5334/cstp.15

Benson, R. (2013). *Shaping immigration news*. Cambridge: Cambridge University Press.

Benson, R., & Neveu, E. (2005). Introduction: Field theory as a work in progress. In R. Benson & E. Neveu (Eds.), *Bourdieu and the journalistic field* (pp. 1–27). Malden, MA: Polity Books.

Berger, G. (2012). Empowering the youth as citizen journalists: A South African experience. In M. Wall (Ed.), *Citizen journalism: Valuable, useless or dangerous?* (pp. 55–69). New York: IDebate Press.

Bhat, P. (2018). Advertisements in the age of hyper partisan media: Breitbart's #DumpKellogs campaign. In R. E. Gutsche Jr. (Ed.), *The Trump presidency, journalism, and democracy* (pp. 192–204). New York: Routledge.

Birchall, M. (2017). Situating participatory art between process and practice: The art of taking part. *Arken Bulletin, 7*, 56–74.

Bishop, C. (2012). *Artificial hells: Participatory art and the politics of spectatorship*. New York: Verso Books.

Bloom, J. A. (2012, October 29). Breitbart and the closing of the tech gap. *The American Conservative*. Retrieved from www.theamericanconservative.com/2012/10/29/breitbart-and-the-closing-of-the-tech-gap

Bock, M. A. (2012). Citizen video journalists and authority in narrative: Reviving the role of the witness. *Journalism, 13*(5), 639–653.

Bock, M. A. (2016). Film the police! Cop-watching and its embodied narratives. *Journal of Communication, 66*(1), 13–34.

Bonney, R., Shirk, J. L., Phillips, T. B., Wiggins, A., Ballard, H. L., Miller-Rushing, A. J., & Parrish, J. K. (2014, March 28). Next steps for citizen science. *Science, 343*(6178), 1436–1437.

Borger, M., Van Hoof, A., & Sanders, J. (2016a). Expecting reciprocity: Towards a model of the participants' perspective on participatory journalism. *New Media & Society, 18*(5), 708–725.

Borger, M., Van Hoof, A., & Sanders, J. (2016b). Exploring participatory journalistic content: Objectivity and diversity in five examples of participatory journalism. *Journalism.* https://doi.org/10.1177/1464884916675633

Bossio, D., & Bebawi, S. (2012). Reaping and sowing the news from an Arab Spring: The politicised interaction between traditional and alternative journalistic practitioners. *Global Media Journal – Australian Edition, 6*(2), 1–12.

Bourdieu, P. (1993). *The field of cultural production: Essays on art and literature.* New York: Columbia University Press.

Bourdieu, P. (2005). The political field, the social science field, and the journalistic field. In R. Benson & E. Neveu (Eds.), *Bourdieu and the journalistic field* (pp. 29–47). Malden, MA: Polity Books.

boyd, d. (2017, January 5). Did media literacy fail? *Data & Society.* Retrieved from https://points.datasociety.net/did-media-literacy-backfire-7418c084d88d

Breitbart, A. (2011). *Righteous indignation: Excuse me while I save the world.* New York: Grand Central Publishing.

Canter, L. (2013). The source, the resource and the collaborator: The role of citizen journalism in local UK newspapers. *Journalism, 14*(8), 1091–1109.

Carlson, M. (2015). Introduction: The many boundaries of journalism. In M. Carlson & S. C. Lewis (Eds.), *Boundaries of journalism: Professionalism, practices and participation* (pp. 1–18). New York: Routledge.

Chadha, K., & Steiner, L. (2015). The potential and limitations of citizen journalism initiatives: Chhattisgarh's CGNet Swara. *Journalism Studies, 16*(5), 706–718.

Chang, A. (2018, June 21). Watch: Sinclair forced its TV stations to air pro-Trump propaganda on family separation. *Vox.* Retrieved from www.vox.com/2018/6/21/17488540/sinclair-tv-stations-family-separation-propaganda

Chen, A. (2014, December). Is livestreaming the future of media, or the future of activism? It might be both. A report from Ferguson, and your laptop screen. *New York Magazine.* Retrieved from http://nymag.com/daily/intelligencer/2014/12/livestreaming-the-future-of-media-or-activism.html

Clark, M. (2018). Black Twitter. In D. Freelon, L. Lopez, M. Clark, & S. J. Jackson (Eds.), *How Black Twitter and other social media communities interact with mainstream news* (pp. 36–46). Miami: John S. and James L. Knight Foundation.

Cooper, C. B. (2016). *Citizen science: How ordinary people are changing the face of discovery.* New York: Overlook Press.

Cooper, C. B., Shirk, J. L., & Zuckerberg, B. (2014). The invisible prevalence of citizen science in global research: Migratory birds and climate change. *PLoS ONE, 9*(9). Retrieved from http://journals.plos.org/plosone/article?id=10.1371/journal.pone.0106508

Dahlgren, P. (2016). Professional and citizen journalism: Tensions and complements. In J. C. Alexander, E. B. Breese, & M. Luengo (Eds.), *The crisis of journalism reconsidered* (pp. 247–263). Cambridge: Cambridge University Press.

Davis, S. (2017). Citizen health journalism: Negotiating between political engagement and professional identity in a media training program for healthcare workers. *Journalism Practice, 11*(2–3), 319–335.

Deluca, K. M., & Lawson, S. (2014). Occupy Wall Street and social media sharing after the wake of institutional journalism. In E. Thorsen & S. Allan (Eds.), *Citizen journalism: Global perspectives* (Vol. 2, pp. 361–375). New York: Peter Lang.

Dickinson, J. L., Shirk, J. L., Bonter, D., Bonney, R., Crain, R. L., Martin, J., . . . Purcell, K. (2012). The current state of citizen science as a tool for ecological research and public engagement. *Frontiers in Ecology and the Environment, 10*(6), 291–297.

D'Ignazio, C., & Zuckerman, E. (2017). Are we citizen scientists, citizen sensors or something else entirely? In B. S. De Abreu, P. Mihailidis, A. Y. L. Lee, J. Melki, & J. McDougall (Eds.), *International handbook of media literacy education* (pp. 193–210). New York: Routledge.

Domingo, D. (2011). Managing audience participation: Practices, workflows, strategies. In J. B. Singer, A. Hermida, D. Domingo, A. Heinonen, S. Paulussen, T. Quandt, . . . M. Vujnovic (Eds.), *Participatory journalism: Guarding open gates at online newspapers* (pp. 76–95). Malden, MA: John Wiley & Sons.

Domingo, D., & Le Cam, F. (2016). Journalistic role performance beyond professional news media. In C. Mellado, L. Hellmueller, & W. Donsbach (Eds.), *Journalistic role performance: Concepts, contexts, and methods* (pp. 155–170). New York: Routledge.

Durham, F. (2018). The origins of Trump's alternative reality. A brief history of the Breitbart effect. In R. E. Gutsche Jr. (Ed.), *The Trump presidency, journalism, and democracy* (pp. 181–191). New York: Routledge.

Eitzel, M. V., Cappadonna, J. L., Santos-Lang, C., Duerr, R. E., Virapongse, A., West, S. E., . . . Jiang, Q. (2017). Citizen science terminology matters: Exploring key terms. *Citizen Science: Theory and* Practice, *2*(1), 1–20.

Eldridge II, S. E. (2016). The digital journalist: The journalistic field, boundaries and disquieting change. In B. Franklin & S. E. Eldridge II (Eds.), *The Routledge companion to digital journalism studies* (pp. 44–54). New York: Routledge.

Eldridge II, S. E. (2018). *Online journalism from the periphery: Interloper media and the journalistic field.* New York: Routledge.

Eric Poemoceah arrested on Facebook Live at DAPL protest. (n.d.). *Newson6.com.* Retrieved from www.newson6.com/clip/13125680/eric-poemoceah-arrested-on-facebook-live-at-dapl-protest

Faris, R., Roberts, H., Etling, B., Bourassa, N., Zuckerman, E., & Benkler, Y. (2017, August). *Partisanship, propaganda, and disinformation: Online media and the 2016 US presidential election.* Berkman Klein Center Research Publication. Retrieved from https://ssrn.com/abstract=3019414

Finkelpearl, T. (2014). Participatory art. In M. Kelly (Ed.), *Encyclopedia of aesthetics* (pp. 1–8). New York: Oxford University Press.

Fiorella, G., & Leroy, A. (2018, May 13). Was Óscar Pérez murdered? You could help us find out. *New York Times.* Retrieved from www.nytimes.com/2018/05/13/opinion/oscar-perez-venezuela-forensic-architecture.html

Fisher, M., Cox, J. W., & Hermann, P. (2016). Pizzagate: From rumor, to hashtag, to gunfire in D.C. *The Washington Post.* Retrieved from www.washingtonpost.com/local/pizzagate-from-rumor-to-hashtag-to-gunfire-in-dc/2016/12/06/4c7def50-bbd4-11e6-94ac-3d324840106c_story.html?utm_term=.207d6eae98fd

Framke, C. (2017, October 3). The opposition with Jordan Klepper is an unfocused satire of "alt-media" at its most hyperbolic. *Vox.* Retrieved from www.vox.com/fall-tv/2017/10/3/16387536/jordan-klepper-the-opposition-comedy-central-review

Franco, C. (2017, March 12). How Standing Rock birthed a new generation of independent left-wing media. *Vice*. Retrieved from https://www.vice.com/en_us/article/xyka5j/how-standing-rock-birthed-a-new-generation-of-independent-left-wing-media

Freelon, D., Lopez, L., Clark, M., & Jackson, S. J. (2018). *How Black Twitter and other social media communities interact with mainstream news*. Miami: John S. and James L. Knight Foundation.

Gabler, N. (1995). *Winchell: Gossip, power and the culture of celebrity*. New York: Vintage Books.

Gerson, D., Chen, N. T. N., Wenzel, A., Ball-Rokeach, S., & Parks, M. (2017). From audience to reporter: Recruiting and training community members at a participatory news site serving a multiethnic city. *Journalism Practice*, *11*(2–3), 336–354.

Gillespie, M. (2013). BBC Arabic, social media and citizen production: An experiment in digital democracy before the Arab Spring. *Theory, Culture & Society*, *30*(4), 92–130.

Gold, M. (2017, March 17). The Mercers and Stephen Bannon: How a populist power base was funded and built. *The Washington Post*. Retrieved from www.washingtonpost.com/graphics/politics/mercer-bannon/?tid=a_inl_manual

Goldstein, P. (2011, March 18). Tracing the showbiz roots of James O'Keefe's NPR sting. *Los Angeles Times*. Retrieved from http://latimesblogs.latimes.com/the_big_picture/2011/03/the-news-me . . . ames-okeefe-the-wily-troublemaker-whose-hidden-camera-sting-co.html

Goodwin, D., Pope, C., Mort, M., & Smith, A. (2005). Access, boundaries and their effects: Legitimate participation in anesthesia. *Sociology of Health & Illness*, *27*(6), 855–871.

Gowing, N. (2014). Beyond journalism: The new public information space. In E. Thorsen & S. Allan (Eds.), *Citizen journalism: Global perspectives* (Vol. 2, pp. 303–320). New York: Peter Lang.

Haimson, O. L., & Tang, J. C. (2017, May). *What makes live events engaging on Facebook Live, Periscope, and Snapchat*. Proceedings of the 2017 CHI Conference on Human Factors in Computing Systems (pp. 48–60). ACM.

Haklay, M. (2012). Citizen science and volunteered geographic information: Overview and typology of participation. In D. Sui, S. Elwood, & M. Goodchild (Eds.), *Crowdsourcing geographic knowledge: Volunteered Geographic Information (VGI) in theory and practice* (pp. 105–122). Dordrecht: Springer.

Hanks, W. (1991/2003). Forward. In J. Lave & E. Wenger (Eds.), *Situated learning: Legitimate peripheral participation* (pp. 13–24). Cambridge: Cambridge University Press.

Hannity, S. (2011, April 18). Andrew Breitbart on mission to save world with citizen journalism. *Fox News*. Retrieved from www.foxnews.com/transcript/2011/04/18/andrew-breitbart-on-mission-to-save-world-with-citizen-journalism.html

Harrison, J. (2010). User-generated content and gatekeeping at the BBC hub. *Journalism Studies*, *11*(2), 243–256.

Harte, D., Williams, A., & Turner, J. (2017). Reciprocity and the hyperlocal journalist. *Journalism Practice*, *11*(2–3), 160–176.

Hartog, K. (2012, March 6). Breitbart.com editor-in-chief: "Andrew's legacy is citizen journalism". *Culver City Patch*. Retrieved from https://patch.com/users/kelly-hartog-2

Hawe, A. (2017, December 8). Local citizen journalism initiative creates impact. *Community News Commons*. Retrieved from www.communitynewscommons.org/our-neighbourhoods/local-citizen-journalism-initiative-creates-impact/

Hermida, A. (2015). Nothing but the truth: Redrafting the journalistic boundary of verification. In M. Carlson & S. C. Lewis (Eds.), *Boundaries of journalism: Professionalism, practices and participation* (pp. 37–50). New York: Routledge.

Hermida, A. (2016). Twitter, breaking the news and hybridity in journalism. In B. Franklin & S. E. Eldridge II (Eds.), *The Routledge companion to digital journalism studies* (pp. 407–416). New York: Routledge.

Hewitt, A., & Jordan, M. (2017, June 21–23). *The kiosks of the free art collective: Understanding social art practice and opinion formation for new models of collaboration.* ETHNOARTS – Ethnographic Explorations of the Arts and Education, University of Porto, Portugal.

Hing, J. (2011, March 8). DREAMers come out: "I'm undocumented, unafraid, and unapologetic". *Colorlines*. Retrieved from www.colorlines.com/articles/dreamers-come-out-im-undocumented-unafraid-and-unapologetic

Hockin, S. M., & Brunson, R. K. (2018). The revolution might not be televised (but it will be lived streamed): Future directions for research on police – minority relations. *Race and Justice*, *8*(3), 199–215.

Hohmann, J. (2010, September 12). Breitbart dials up a TV dream. *Politico*. Retrieved from www.politico.com/story/2010/09/breitbart-dials-up-a-tv-dream-042044

Hung, C-L. (2015). Citizen journalists as an empowering community for change. In G. D. Rawnsley & M. T. Rawnsley (Eds.), *Routledge handbook of Chinese media* (pp. 161–177). New York: Routledge.

Hung-lo, S. (2012). Public television service and its citizen journalism initiative in Taiwan. In M. Wall (Ed.), *Citizen journalism: Valuable, useless or dangerous?* (pp. 71–81). New York: IDebate Press.

Husband, C. (2005). Minority ethnic media as communities of practice: Professionalism and identity politics in interaction. *Journal of Ethnic and Migration Studies*, *31*(3), 461–479.

Jackson, S. J., & Welles, B. F. (2016). #Ferguson is everywhere: Initiators in emerging counterpublic networks. *Information, Communication & Society*, *19*(3), 397–418.

Jenkins, H., Shresthova, S., Gamber-Thompson, L., Kligler-Vilenchik, N., & Zimmerman, A. (2016). *By any media necessary: The new youth activism*. New York: New York University Press.

Johnson, J. (2018). The self-radicalization of white men: "fake news" and the affective networking of paranoia. *Communication Culture & Critique*, *11*(1), 100–115.

Jönsson, A. M., & Örnebring, H. (2011). User-generated content and the news: Empowerment of citizens or interactive illusion? *Journalism Practice*, *5*(2), 127–144.

Karlsson, M. (2011). Flourishing but restrained: The evolution of participatory journalism in Swedish online news, 2005–2009. *Journalism Practice*, *5*(1), 68–84.

Karlsson, M., Bergström, A., Clerwall, C., & Fast, K. (2015). Participatory journalism – the (r)evolution that wasn't: Content and user behavior in Sweden 2007–2013. *Journal of Computer–Mediated Communication, 20*(3), 295–311.

Kew, B. (2017, Feb. 23). Project Veritas offers $10,000 for evidence of media corruption. *Breitbart*. Retrieved from www.breitbart.com/big-government/2017/02/23/project-veritas-offers-10000-for-evidence-of-media-corruption/

Killelea, E. (2017, April 28). Alex Jones' custody trial: 10 WTF moments. *Rolling Stone*. Retrieved from www.rollingstone.com/culture/culture-news/alex-jones-custody-trial-10-wtf-moments-108404/

Kim, Y., & Lowrey, W. (2015). Who are citizen journalists in the social media environment? Personal and social determinants of citizen journalism activities. *Digital Journalism, 3*(2), 298–314.

Kreiss, D. (2018). The media are about identity, not information. In P. J. Boczkowski & Z. Papacharissi (Eds.), *Trump and the media* (pp. 93–100). Boston: MIT Press.

Kus, M., Eberwein, T., Porlezza, C., & Splendore, S. (2017). Training or improvisation? Citizen journalists and their educational backgrounds – a comparative view. *Journalism Practice, 11*(2–3), 355–372.

Lakshmanan, I. (2017, April 26). Breitbart struggles to define its role in Trump era: Bad boy, watchdog or lapdog? *Poynter*. Retrieved from www.poynter.org/news/breitbart-struggles-define-its-role-trump-era-bad-boy-watchdog-or-lapdog

Lal, J. (2013, March 28). How queer undocumented youth built the immigrant rights movement. *Huffington Post*. Retrieved from www.huffingtonpost.com/prerna-lal/how-queer-undocumented_b_2973670.html

Lave, J., & Wenger, E. (1991/2003). *Situated learning: Legitimate peripheral participation*. Cambridge: Cambridge University Press.

Lee, T. (2012, June 16). Top ten quotes from Sarah Palin's right online address. *Breitbart*. Retrieved from www.breitbart.com/big-government/2012/06/16/sarah-palin-s-top-ten-quotes-from-raucous-right-online-speech/

Lee, T. (2015, March 9). Legacy media's Ron Fournier: Hillary doesn't realize internet has eliminated MSM gatekeepers, lets people "see through the lies." *Breitbart*. Retrieved from www.breitbart.com/big-journalism/2015/03/09/legacy-medias-ron-fournier-hillary-doesnt-realize-internet-has-eliminated-msm-gatekeepers-lets-people-see-through-the-lies/

Lewis, E. (2009, September 20). The ACORN witch hunt; voter-registration success spurs unfair attack. *New York Daily News*. Retrieved from Pro-Quest database.

Lewis, S. C. (2012). The tension between professional control and open participation: Journalism and its boundaries. *Information, Communication & Society, 15*(6), 836–866.

Lewis, S. C. (2015). Epilogue. In M. Carlson & S. Lewis (Eds.), *Boundaries of journalism: Professionalism, practices and participation* (pp. 218–228). New York: Routledge.

Lewis, S. C., Holton, A. E., & Coddington, M. (2016). From participation to reciprocity in the journalist-audience relationship. In C. Peters & M. Broersma (Eds.), *Rethinking journalism again: Societal role and public relevance in a digital age* (pp. 161–174). New York: Routledge.

Li, Y., & Hellmueller, L. (2016). A longitudinal study of CNN's integration of participatory journalism. In S. E. Eldridge II & B. Franklin (Eds.), *The Routledge companion to digital journalism studies* (pp. 335–344). New York: Routledge.

Lisenby, A. (2017, September 22). Live streamers hit the streets of St. Louis along with protesters. *St. Louis Today*. Retrieved from www.stltoday.com/news/local/metro/live-streamers-hit-the-streets-of-st-louis-along-with/article_36f19a65-c5a6-506a-a26b-98bb13ddfe10.html

Literat, I. (2012). The work of art in the age of mediated participation: Crowdsourced art and collective creativity. *International Journal of Communication, 6,* 2962–2984.

Literat, I. (2016). Interrogating participation across disciplinary boundaries: Lessons from political philosophy, cultural studies, art, and education. *New Media & Society, 18*(8), 1787–1803.

Lozano, D. (2017, December 20). Maduro ordena al ejército que embista a "plomo" contra "Rambo Pérez" y acusa a Miami de gestar la toma de un cuartel. *El Mundo*. Retrieved from www.elmundo.es/internacional/2017/12/20/5a39b3a0268e3ec64 28b45e7.html

Luce, A., Jackson, D., & Thorsen, E. (2017). Citizen journalism at the margins. *Journalism Practice, 11*(2–3), 266–284.

Mahrouse, G. (2012). The compelling story of the white/western activist in the war zone: Examining race, neutrality, and exceptionalism in citizen journalism. In M. Wall (Ed.), *Citizen journalism: Valuable, useless or dangerous?* (pp. 163–179). New York: IDebate Press.

Making news through trolling. (n.d.). *Mike Cernovich*. Southern Poverty Law Center. Retrieved from www.splcenter.org/fighting-hate/extremist-files/individual/mike-cernovich

Mano, W. (2010). Between citizen and vigilante journalism: *ZimDaily*'s fair deal campaign and the Zimbabwe crisis. *Communicare: Journal for Communication Sciences in Southern Africa, 1,* 57–70.

Maracci, C. (2016, October 14). *Sauti ya Mtaa*, a new online platform to reinvent citizen journalism. *Medium*. Retrieved from https://medium.com/journalism-innovation/sauti-ya-mtaa-a-new-online-platform-to-reinvent-citizen-journalism-a314a232ff24

Marathe, M., O'Neill, J., Pain, P., & Thies, W. (2015, May). *Revisiting CGNet Swara and its impact in rural India*. Proceedings of the Seventh International Conference on Information and Communication Technologies and Development.

Martini, M. (2018). Online distant witnessing and live-streaming activism: Emerging differences in the activation of networked publics. *New Media & Society*. Online first, 1–8.

Marwick, A., & Lewis, R. (2017). Media manipulation and dis-information online. *Data and Society*. Retrieved from https://datasociety.net/output/media-manipulation-and-disinfo-online/

Marx, G. (2010, February 4). The ethics of undercover journalism: Why journalists get squeamish over James O'Keefe's tactics. *Columbia Journalism Review*. Retrieved from www.cjr.org/campaign_desk/the_ethics_of_undercover_journalism.php?page=all

Masri, B. (2014, October 28). *In Ferguson, I am reminded of Palestine.* American Friends Service Committee. Retrieved from www.afsc.org/friends/ferguson-i-am-reminded-palestine

Masters, K., Oh, E. Y., Cox, J., Simmons, B., Lintott, C., Graham, G., Greenhill, A., & Holmes, K. (2016). Science learning via participation in online citizen science. *Journal of Science Communication, 15*(3), 1–33.

Matsaganis, M. D., & Katz, V. S. (2014). How ethnic media producers constitute their communities of practice: An ecological approach. *Journalism, 15*(7), 926–944.

McLaughlin, A. (2017, May 9). PizzaGate conspiracist attends white house press briefing: Who is he? *Mediate.* Retrieved from www.mediaite.com/online/pizzagate-conspiracist-attends-white-house-press-briefing-who-is-he/

Miller, J. (2016). Activism vs. antagonism: Socially engaged art from Bourriaud to Bishop and beyond. *Field: A Journal of Socially Engaged Art Criticism, 3,* 165–183.

Mugar, G., Østerlund, C., Hassman, K. D., Crowston, K., & Jackson, C. B. (2014, February). *Planet hunters and seafloor explorers: Legitimate peripheral participation through practice proxies in online citizen science.* Proceedings of the 17th ACM conference on Computer supported cooperative work & social computing (pp. 109–119).

Nagle, A. (2017). *Kill all normies: Online culture wars from 4chan and Tumblr to Trump and the alt-right.* Alresfor, Hants: John Hunt Publishing.

NavigationArts' next generation web design continues Andrew Breitbart's vision. (2012, August 23). *Business Wire.* ProQuest Database.

Nazaryan, A. (2018, January 17). James O'Keefe: Meet the man who makes the fake news. *Newsweek.* Retrieved from www.newsweek.com/2018/02/02/james-okeefe-project-veritas-american-pravda-fake-news-781964.html

Nicey, J. (2016). Semi-professional amateurs. In T. Witschge, C. W. Anderson, D. Domingo, & A. Hermida (Eds.), *The Sage handbook of digital journalism* (pp. 222–235). London: Sage.

Nip, J. Y. (2006). Exploring the second phase of public journalism. *Journalism Studies, 7*(2), 212–236.

O'Harrow, R. Jr. (2017, December 2). Project veritas received $1.7 million last year from charity associated with the Koch brothers. *The Washington Post.* Retrieved from http://wapo.st/2ApzV58?tid=ss_tw&utm_term=.b62baf92d40c

O'Kane, C. (2018, June 28). Woman dubbed "Pool Patrol Paula" charged with assaulting black teen at swimming pool. *CBS News.* Retrieved from www.cbsnews.com/news/stephanie-sebby-strempel-pool-patrol-paula-video-woman-allegedly-assaulting-black-teen-south-carolina-community-pool/

O'Keefe, J. (2013). *Breakthrough: Our guerilla war to expose fraud and save democracy.* New York: Threshold Editions, Simon Schuster.

O'Keefe, J. (2018). *American Pravda: My fight for truth in the era of fake news.* New York: St. Martin's Press.

Oney, S. (2010, April 5). Citizen Breitbart: Polarizing and profane, Andrew Breitbart is fast becoming the most powerful right-wing force on the web. *Time,* 35–37.

Pain, P. (2017). Educate. Empower. Revolt: Framing citizen journalism as a creator of social movements. *Journalism Practice,* 1–18.

74   *References*

Palma, B. (2018, March 23). *How to recognize online hoaxes in an era of fake news.* Lecture presented at JACC State Convention in Burbank Marriott Convention Center, Burbank.

Palmer, R. (2017). *Becoming the news: How ordinary people respond to the media spotlight.* New York: Columbia University Press.

Pantti, M., & Andén-Papadopoulos, K. (2011). Transparency and trustworthiness: Strategies for incorporating amateur photography into news discourse. In K. Andén-Papadopoulos & M. Pantti (Eds.), *Amateur images and global news* (pp. 99–112). Chicago, IL: Intellect, The University of Chicago Press.

Papacharisis, Z. (2015). Affective publics and structures of storytelling: Sentiment, events and mediality. *Information, Communication & Society, 19*(3), 307–324.

Phillips, T. B., Bonney, R., & Shirk, J. L. (2012). What is our impact? Toward a unifying framework for evaluating outcomes of citizen science participation. In J. L. Dickinson & R. Bonney (Eds.), *Citizen science: Public participation in environmental research* (pp. 82–95). Cornell: Cornell University Press.

Phillips, T. B., Ferguson, M., Minarchek, M., Porticella, N., & Bonney, R. (2014). *User's guide for evaluating learning outcomes in citizen science.* Ithaca, NY: Cornell Lab of Ornithology.

Phillips, W. (2018). The oxygen of amplification. *Data & Society.* Retrieved from https://datasociety.net/wp-content/uploads/2018/05/FULLREPORT_Oxygen_of_Amplification_DS.pdf

Pollack, J. (2017, April 13). Russian disinformation technology. *MIT Technology Review.* Retrieved form www.technologyreview.com/s/604084/russian-disinformation-technology/

Prado, P. (2017). Mapping citizen journalism and the promise of digital inclusion: A perspective from the global South. *Global Media and Communication, 13*(2), 87–104.

Rahimi, S. (2015, March 27). How we reported #Ferguson using only mobile phones. *AJ+.* Retrieved from https://medium.com/aj-story-behind-the-story/how-we-reported-ferguson-using-only-mobile-phones-2a6686c89c71

Rains, S. (2017, February 23). Comanche protester arrested in Dakota. *The Lawton Constitution.* Retrieved from www.swoknews.com/local/comanche-protester-arrested-dakota

Reese, S. D., & Dai, J. (2009). Citizen journalism in the global news arena: China's new media critics. In S. Allan & E. Thorsen (Eds.), *Citizen journalism: Global perspectives* (pp. 221–231). New York: Peter Lang.

Rhodan, M. (2017, April 17). President Trump's favorite conspiracy theorist is just "playing a character," his lawyer says. *Time.* Retrieved from http://time.com/4743025/alex-jones-infowars-divorce-donald-trump/

Richardson, A. V. (2017). Bearing witness while black: Theorizing African American mobile journalism after Ferguson. *Digital Journalism, 5*(6), 673–698.

Rirkrit Tiravanija. (n.d.). *Guggenheim.* Retrieved from www.guggenheim.org/artwork/artist/rirkrit-tiravanija

Robinson, S. (2009). "If you had been with us": Mainstream press and citizen journalists jockey for authority over the collective memory of Hurricane Katrina. *New Media & Society, 11*(5), 795–814.

Robinson, S. (2010). Traditionalists vs. convergers: Textual privilege, boundary work, and the journalist – audience relationship in the commenting policies of online news sites. *Convergence*, *16*(1), 125–143.

Robinson, S. (2015). Redrawing borders from within: Commenting on news stories as boundary work. In M. Carlson & S. C. Lewis (Eds.), *Boundaries of journalism: Professionalism, practices and participation* (pp. 152–167). New York: Routledge.

Robinson, S., & DeShano, C. (2011). "Anyone can know": Citizen journalism and the interpretive community of the mainstream press. *Journalism*, *12*(8), 963–982.

Robinson, S., & Schwartz, M. L. (2014). The activist as citizen journalist. In E. Thorsen & S. Allan (Eds.), *Citizen journalism: Global perspectives* (Vol. 2, pp. 377–389). New York: Peter Lang.

Roche, J., & Davis, N. (2017). Citizen science: An emerging professional field united in truth-seeking. *Journal of Science Communication, 16*(4), 1–6.

Rodríguez, C. (2011). *Citizens' media against armed conflict: Disrupting violence in Colombia*. Minneapolis: University of Minnesota Press.

Rodríguez, C. (2014). A Latin American approach to citizen journalism. In Thorsen, E., & Allan, S. (Eds.), *Citizen journalism: global perspectives*, vol. 2 (pp. 199–210). New York: Peter Lang.

Roig-Franzia, M. (2016, November 16). How Alex Jones, conspiracy theorist extraordinaire, got Donald Trump's ear. *The Washington Post*. Retrieved from www.washingtonpost.com/lifestyle/style/how-alex-jones-conspiracy-theorist-extraordinaire-got-donald-trumps-ear/2016/11/17/583dc190-ab3e-11e6-8b45-f8e493f06fcd_story.html

Rosenberry, J., & St. John, B. (Eds.). (2009). Introduction: Public journalism values in an age of media fragmentation. In J. Rosenberry & B. St. John (Eds.), *Public journalism 2.0: The promise and reality of a citizen engaged press* (pp. 1–6). New York: Routledge.

Russell, A. (2016). *Journalism as activism: Recoding media power*. Malden, MA: Polity Books.

Sambrook, R. (2009). Citizen journalism. In J. Owen & H. Purdey (Eds.), *International news reporting: Frontlines and deadlines* (pp. 220–242). Malden, MA: Wiley-Blackwell.

Schmitz Weiss, A., & Domingo, D. (2010). Innovation processes in online newsrooms as actor-networks and communities of practice. *New Media & Society, 12*(7), 1156–1171.

Scott, D. T. (2007). Pundits in muckrakers clothing: Political blogs and the 2004 presidential election. In M. Tremayne (Ed.), *Blogging, citizenship, and the future of media* (pp. 39–58). New York: Routledge.

Singer, J. (2015). Out of bounds: Professional norms as boundary markers. In M. Carlson & S. C. Lewis (Eds.), *Boundaries of journalism: Professionalism, practices and participation* (pp. 21–36). New York: Routledge.

Sommer, W. (2018, June 27). Jack Posobiec and Laura Loomer fight for credit over Vegas shooting conspiracy theory. *The Daily Beast*. Retrieved from http://libproxy.csun.edu/login?url=https://search-proquest-com.libproxy.csun.edu/docview/2059834045?accountid=7285

Sound recording: A GuardianWitness guide to making great video. (n.d.). *Guardian-Witness*. Retrieved from https://witness.theguardian.com/tips-and-tricks

Splichal, S., & Dahlgren, P. (2016). Journalism between de-professionalisation and democratisation. *European Journal of Communication, 31*(1), 5–18.

St. Félix, D. (2018, July 21). The summer of Coupon Carl, Permit Patty, and the videos that turn white privilege into mockable memes. *The New Yorker*. Retrieved from https://www.newyorker.com/culture/culture-desk/the-summer-of-coupon-carl-permit-patty-and-the-videos-that-turn-cop-callers-into-mockable-memes

Stallings, S., & Mauldin, B. (2016). *Public engagement in the arts: A review of recent literature*. Los Angeles: Los Angeles County Arts Commission.

Stelter, B. (2014, November 17). Live-streamers vs. reporters in Ferguson. *CNN*. Retrieved from www.youtube.com/watch?v=MJBbG4ZE2RY&t=124s

Stilgoe, J. (2016, November 8). Is citizen science the future of research or a recipe for bad science? *The Guardian*. Retrieved from www.theguardian.com/science/political-science/2016/nov/08/is-citizen-science-the-future-of-research-or-a-recipe-for-bad-science

Sullivan, B. (2017, March 7). Bellingcat wants your help to debunk fake news. *Motherboard*. Retrieved from https://motherboard.vice.com/en_us/article/78qbqy/bellingcat-wants-your-help-to-debunk-fake-news

Svitek, P. (2013, May 14). Conservative activist James O'Keefe talks citizen journalism at "Hating Breitbart" screening. *The Daily Northwestern*. Retrieved from https://dailynorthwestern.com/2013/05/14/campus/conservative-activist-james-okeefe-talks-citizen-journalism-at-hating-breitbart-screening/

Taub, A., & Fisher, M. (2018, April 21). Where countries are tinderboxes and Facebook is a match. *The New York Times*. Retrieved from www.nytimes.com/2018/04/21/world/asia/facebook-sri-lanka-riots.html

The 2016 election emboldened dangerous "citizen journalist" vigilantes. (2016, December 23). *Media matters*. Retrieved from www.mediamatters.org/blog/2016/12/23/2016-election-emboldened-dangerous-citizen-journalist-vigilantes/214880

Thorburn, E. D. (2014). Social media, subjectivity, and surveillance: Moving on from occupy, the rise of live streaming video. *Communication and Critical/Cultural Studies, 11*(1), 52–63.

Thorsen, E., & Allan, S. (Eds.). (2014). *Citizen journalism: Global perspectives* (Vol. 2). New York: Peter Lang.

Ungar, R. (2013, March 8). James O'Keefe pays $100,000 to ACORN employee he smeared; conservative media yawns. *Forbes*. Retrieved from www.forbes.com/sites/rickungar/2013/03/08/james-okeefe-pays-100000-to-acorn-employee-he-smeared-conservative-media-yawns/#2bb1b68214bd

Venezuela says rebel pilot Oscar Perez killed in raid. (2018, January 17). *France 24*. Retrieved from www.france24.com/en/20180117-venezuela-says-rebel-pilot-oscar-perez-killed-raid

Venezuelan rebel leader Oscar Perez records his last stand. (2018, January 16). *The New York Times*. Retrieved from www.youtube.com/watch?v=8bC6rwTATZI

Voices on Ferguson & police accountability: Bassem Masri (2015, Aug. 19). *Amnesty International*. Retrieved from www.youtube.com/watch?v=qqRihbu16Mk

Wahl-Jorgensen, K. (2015). Resisting epistemologies of user-generated content? Cooptation, segregation and the boundaries of journalism. In M. Carlson & S. C. Lewis (Eds.), *Boundaries of journalism: Professionalism, practices and partici-pation* (pp. 169–185). New York: Routledge.

Waisbord, S. (2014). Citizen journalism, development and social change: Hype and hope. In E. Thorsen & S. Allan (Eds.), *Citizen journalism: Global perspectives* (Vol. 2, pp. 185–197). New York: Peter Lang.

Wall, M. (2012). *Citizen journalism: Valuable, useless or dangerous?* New York: IDebate Press.

Wall, M. (2015). Citizen journalism: A retrospective on what we know, an agenda for what we don't. *Digital Journalism*, *3*(6), 797–813.

Wall, M. (2016). Citizen journalism: Connections, contradictions, and conflicts. In B. Franklin & S. E. Eldridge II (Eds.), *The Routledge companion to digital jour-nalism studies* (pp. 235–243). New York: Routledge.

Wall, M. (2017). Mapping citizen and participatory journalism: In newsrooms, classrooms and beyond. *Journalism Practice*, *11*(2–3), 134–141.

Wall, M. (2018). How and why pop-up news ecologies come into being. In S. E. Eldridge II & B. Franklin (Eds.), *The Routledge handbook of developments in digital journalism studies* (pp. 375–386). New York: Routledge.

Wall, M., & el Zahed, S. (2015). Embedding content from Syrian citizen journalists: The rise of the collaborative news clip. *Journalism*, *16*(2), 163–180.

Weigel, D. (2017, February 3). The left jousts with James O'Keefe. *The Washing-ton Post*. Retrieved from https://wapo.st/2jMAV9A?tid=ss_mail&utm_term=. bece170146b7.

Wenger, E. (1998a). *Communities of practice: Learning, meaning, and identity*. Cambridge: Cambridge University Press.

Wenger, E. (1998b). Communities of practice: Learning as a social system. *Systems Thinker*, *5*(4), 1–10.

What the media can learn from James O'Keefe. (2011, March 18). *On the Media*. Retrieved from www.wnyc.org/story/133115-what-the-media-can-learn-from-james-okeefe/

Why work together? (n.d.). *Citizen Science Alliance*. Retrieved from www.citizen sciencealliance.org/philosophy.html

Williams, B. A., & Delli Carpini, M. X. (2000). Unchained reaction: The collapse of media gatekeeping and the Clinton – Lewinsky scandal. *Journalism*, *1*(1), 61–85.

Williams, C. (2015, July 9). Why I founded #CharlestonSyllabus after the Charles-ton shooting. *PBS News Hour*. Retrieved from www.pbs.org/newshour/education/founded-charlestonsyllabus-charleston-shooting

Williamson, E. (2018, March 26). *How a UVA Law-trained team helped win jus-tice for DeAndre Harris*. Retrieved from www.law.virginia.edu/news/201803/how-uva-law-trained-team-helped-win-justice-deandre-harris

Willis, E., & Painter, C. (2016). Race prominent feature in coverage of Trayvon Martin. *Newspaper Research Journal*, *37*(2), 180–195.

Yousuf, M., & Taylor, M. (2017). Helping Syrians tell their story to the world: Train-ing Syrian citizen journalists through connective journalism. *Journalism Prac-tice*, *11*(2–3), 302–318.

Index

80   *Index*